INDIA

INDIA

BY

JOHN FINNEMORE

GYAN

Published by

Gyan Publishing House
5, Ansari Road
Daryaganj, New Delhi-110002
Phone: 011-47034999, 9811692060
E-mail: books@gyanbooks.com

Distribution Network
gyanbooks.com
India, USA, Canada, UK, Australia, France

ISBN: 978-81-212-8780-7 (PB)
First Published, 1910

2nd Impression 2023

Printed at: Gyan Press, Delhi.

INDIA
Author: John Finnemore

A TAILOR AT WORK. *Page 1.*

PEEPS AT MANY LANDS

INDIA

BY

JOHN FINNEMORE

WITH TWELVE FULL-PAGE ILLUSTRATIONS

BY

MORTIMER MENPES

LONDON
ADAM AND CHARLES BLACK
1910

CONTENTS

EX-LIBRIS
Lucia K. Sherman
San Francisco

LIST OF ILLUSTRATIONS

BY MORTIMER MENPES

Sketch-Map of India on page vii.

SKETCH-MAP OF INDIA.

A BUSY BAZAAR. *Chapter XIV.*

INDIA

CHAPTER I

THE GATEWAY OF INDIA

To the vast majority of European travellers Bombay is the gateway of India. It is here they get their first glimpse of the bewildering variety of races, of colours, of types, of customs, which make up India. After the journey through the Suez Canal, and the long run across the Arabian Sea, the traveller is very glad to spend a day or two at Bombay, gaining first impressions of this new, strange country. He may be interested in the fine new buildings of the modern town, or he may not; he is certain to be interested in the native quarter.

Here he gets his first glimpse of that great feature of Indian life, the bazaar—rows and rows of narrow streets filled with shops and crowds. The shops are small booths, often built of mud, or archways, or, again, are mere holes in a wall. Everything is open to full view; there are neither windows nor doors. The merchant or shopkeeper squats beside his goods; the artisan does his work in sight of the passers-by. The crowds are stranger than the shops. Here you may see

Hindoos, Parsees, Burmese, Singhalese, Lascars, Moslems, Arabs, Somalis, Jews of many countries, Turks, Chinese, Japanese, and a score of other nations. Amid the throng of many colours move white people from every land of Europe, and the babel of tongues is as astonishing as the mingling of costumes.

Here is struck at once the note of colour which enlivens every street scene in India. The people wear robes of every shade, and turbans or caps of every hue —black, white, red, green, yellow, purple, pink, every colour of the rainbow—and a hundred shades of every colour meet and mingle as the crowds flow to and fro.

Where there is an open space the snake-charmer squats beside his cobras, playing on his strange pipe, and putting his venomous pets through their tricks; or a conjurer is causing a mango-plant to spring up and put forth fruit from apparently a little barren heap of earth. Busy Indian coolies, naked save for a dirty turban and a wisp of cotton cloth round the loins, hurry along with water-skins, and the skins, filled with water, take roughly the shape of the sheep or goat which had once filled them with flesh and bones. Other coolies are driving queer little carts drawn by a pair of tiny, mild-eyed, hump-backed oxen; and others, again, squat beside the way with their chins on their knees, waiting to be hired.

When it comes to sight-seeing proper, the traveller will visit the island of Elephanta, six miles from the city. Here stands a great temple cut in the solid rock, its roof supported by huge pillars left standing when the chamber was hollowed out. The temple is adorned with colossal figures and carvings of Hindoo gods and of animals. Its excavation must have been a tremendous piece of work, and it is considered that it was carried out some eleven hundred years ago.

Among the crowds of Bombay no people are more distinctive than the Parsees. The Parsees may always be known by the strange head-gear and long coats of the men and by the splendid dresses of the women, who move about as freely as European women, and are not shut up like Hindoo women of the richer classes.

The Parsee man wears on his head a long, high, shiny hat in the form of a cylinder; it has no brim, and is one of the oddest head-coverings that may be seen. In origin he is a Persian, for the Parsees are descended from a race that fled into India from Persia when that land was attacked by the Arabs twelve centuries ago. The Parsee women are dressed very splendidly, because their race is very rich. The Parsee is the banker and money-lender of India. No other native is so clever in trade or amasses wealth so swiftly as a Parsee.

In his religion the most sacred thing is fire, and to him the sun, as the emblem of fire, is the greatest religious symbol. Upon the shore of the bay many Parsees may be seen at evening at their devotions before the setting sun. Each seats himself upon the sand, bows to the sun, taking off his hat and replacing it, and then, with a small brass jar at his side, begins to read prayers from a sacred book, chanting them aloud.

The Parsee reverence for fire is seen in the treatment

of his dead. The Hindoo makes a funeral pyre and burns his dead. Not so the Parsec. He considers that fire is too sacred to use for such a purpose; nor, on the other hand, is he willing to defile the earth by digging a grave. So the Parsee dead are exposed to be torn to pieces and devoured by vultures. Beside the sea there stand five broad low towers, the famous Towers of Silence. In these the bodies of the dead are exposed. One of these is reserved for the use of a wealthy family, one for suicides and those who die by accidental deaths, and three for general use. The towers and the trees around are loaded with huge vultures, which, in a couple of hours, reduce a body to a heap of bones.

CHAPTER II

IN THE LAND OF THE RAJPUTS

RAJPUTANA is the land of the Rajputs, a splendid warrior race of Northern India. In times long gone by the Rajputs held power over the wide plain watered by the Upper Ganges, but seven hundred years ago their Moslem foes drove them westwards into the land still called Rajputana.

The history of the Rajputs is one of battle. They are born fighters. They have taken a share in all the wars which have torn India through all the centuries. They struggled hard against the British power, but now they are good friends of ours, and their Princes rule under British protection.

In the Land of the Rajputs

The history of this fine race is full of stories of romance and chivalry. Nor is the Rajput of to-day inferior to his brave and haughty fathers : " The poorest Rajput retains all his pride of ancestry, often his sole inheritance ; he scorns to hold the plough, or use his lance but on horseback." Of all the brave old stories of Rajput valour and constancy none are more beloved than the tales which hang around the three sacks of Chitore. Thrice was that ancient city seized and plundered by Moslem foes, and never have those terrible days been forgotten. To this day the most binding oath on Rajput lips is when he swears, " By the sin of the sack of Chitore."

Long ago there was a Prince of Chitore named Bhimsi, whose wife, Princess Padmani, was famed far and wide as the most beautiful woman in the world, and as good as she was beautiful. The report of her beauty drew Allah-u-din, a great Moslem warrior, to the walls of Chitore at the head of a powerful army. He demanded to see the face of Padmani, were it only a reflection of her face in a mirror. Prince Bhimsi invited him to a feast, and he saw Padmani. When the feast was over, the Prince escorted Allah-u-din back to his camp. Then the wily Moslem seized the Prince, and sent word to the chiefs of Chitore that, if they wished to see their King again, they must send Padmani to become the wife of Allah-u-din.

Every one in Chitore was aghast at this treacherous deed ; but the Moslem was powerful, and Princess Padmani, with her attendants, set out for the enemy's camp. Slowly the long train of seven hundred litters wound its way from the city, and Padmani was in the hands of Allah-u-din. The Moslem gave permission for Bhimsi and Padmani to take a short farewell of each other, and then was seen a proof of Padmani's wit and Rajput devotion. From out the seven hundred litters sprang, not weeping women, but seven hundred warriors armed to the teeth, while the bearers flung aside their robes, and showed the glittering swords in their strong right hands.

Covered by this devoted bodyguard, Bhimsi and Padmani sprang upon swift horses and reached Chitore in safety. But none else escaped. The noble Rajputs, the flower of Chitore, gave their lives to the last man to save their King and Queen.

Allah-u-din never forgot how he had been foiled. Years passed, and once more he marched against the city set on its rock. No one had ever captured it, and Chitore feared not Allah-u-din until he began to raise a huge mound of earth. He did this by giving gold to all who brought a basketful of earth, and at last he secured a vantage-ground whence he could hurl his missiles into the city, and the end of the siege was near at hand.

Then one night King Bhimsi had a terrible vision, from which he woke in affright. The goddess of Chitore had appeared to him, saying: "If my altar and your throne is to be kept, let twelve who wear the crown die for Chitore."

Now Bhimsi and Padmani had twelve sons. So it was resolved to make them twelve Kings by setting each on the throne for three days. Then the saying of the goddess would be fulfilled, and these twelve must die for Chitore. But when it came to the youngest of the twelve, to Ajeysi, the father's darling, Bhimsi said no. The King called his chieftains together.

"The child shall not die," he said. "He shall go free to recover what was lost. I will be the twelfth to die for Chitore."

"And we will die for Chitore!" cried the warriors. "In bridal robes of saffron and coronets on our heads, we will die for Chitore!"

Then a great plan was made throughout the place: all, men and women, would die for their beloved city. In the vaults and caverns which stretch below the rock a vast funeral pyre was built, and to it came the Rajput women singing, dressed in their festal robes, and glittering in all their jewels. The last to enter the vault of death was Padmani, and when the gate was closed upon her the men knew their turn had come. Setting the little Prince in the midst of a picked band, who had sworn to bear him off in safety, the King led his sons and chieftains to the battle. The gates were flung open, and the warriors, clad in bridal robes, hurled themselves upon the foe: for the bride they sought was death.

When the last had died for Chitore, Allah-u-din entered the city. But it was an empty triumph. Every house, every street, was still and silent, only a wisp of smoke oozed from the vault. This was the first sack of Chitore.

The second sack was in the time of Humayun,

father of Akbar the Great. The ruler of Chitore had died, leaving a baby son to inherit the crown, and when a powerful foe came against the city, the child's mother, Kurnavati, sent messengers to Humayun, saying: "Tell him that he is bracelet-bound brother to me, and that I am hard pressed by a cruel foe."

There is an ancient custom in India by which a woman may choose a bracelet-brother to protect and assist her. She may choose whom she pleases, and she sends him a silken bracelet, called a ram-rukki. It is a mere cord of silk, bound with a tassel, and hung with seven tiny silken tassels—red, orange, yellow, green, blue, indigo, violet, the colours of the rainbow. The man may accept this bracelet or not, as he pleases; but once he has bound it round his wrist, he becomes the bracelet-brother of the sender, and is bound to her service. In return for the bracelet he sends the customary gift of a small breast-bodice.

Now Humayun, the Mogul King, was bracelet-brother to Kurnavati, and when he heard that she was in distress, he hurried to her assistance. But he came too late, and the garrison of Chitore saw that their city must fall. Then they remembered the first sack, and all resolved to die in the same way. Kurnavati succeeded in getting her little son away in safety; then she led the women to the funeral pyre. The men of the garrison were few, for many had fallen, but the gallant handful, clad as before in bridal robes and crowns, dashed upon the foe, and died to the last man, ringed about with heaps of slain.

Although the baby King, Udai Singh, was smuggled

A DISTINGUISHED MAHARAJAH

in safety from Chitore, it was not long before he was in danger again. He was carried off to the palace of his half-brother, Bikramajit, where he lived under the care of his foster-mother, Punnia. One night Punnia heard a terrible uproar, and then the screams of women. Enemies had broken into the palace of Bikramajit. But whose life did they seek above all? Punnia knew, and she saw that Udai Singh was in great danger. How could she save him? There was only one way, a terrible way; but the Rajput woman did not flinch. Two children lay sleeping before her, Udai Singh and her own child. She caught up the baby King and thrust sugared opium into his mouth that he might be lulled into deeper, safer slumber, hid him in a fruit-basket, and gave the precious burden to the hands of a faithful servant. "Fly to the river-bed without the city," she said, "and wait for me there."

Then she flung the rich royal robe over her own sleeping child, and waited for the murderers. In they burst. "The Prince!" they cried. "Where is the Prince?"

With a supreme effort Punnia pointed to the little figure beneath the splendid robe, and hid her face, giving the life of her own child to save that of the little King.

When all was over, and the last funeral rites had been performed over the body of the child whom the conspirators supposed to be the young King, Punnia sought the river-bed. There she found her nursling, and with him she fled over hill and dale, never resting till she gained a strong fortress held by a loyal governor. Into his presence she hastened, and set the child on his knee. "Guard well the life of the King!" she cried, this noble Rajput woman.

The third sack of Chitore happened in the days of Akbar the Great, son of Humayun, who had once hurried to the aid of the city. The Rajputs and the Great Mogul came to blows. Akbar led a powerful army against his foes. This was the last sack, "for the conqueror was of right royal stuff, and knew how to treat brave men. So when the final consummation was once more reached, and thousands of brave men had gone to death by the sword, and thousands of brave women met death by fire, he left the city, levying no ransom, and on the place where his camp had stood raised a white marble tower, from whose top a light might shine to cheer the darkness of Chitore. But a few years afterwards, when in dire distress and riding for his life through an ambush, the man on Akbar's right hand and the man on his left, shielding him from blows, making their swords his shelter, were two of the defeated Rajput generals."

These are stories of long ago. Here is one of times nearer our own, when the English were mastering India. A beautiful Rajput Princess, the Princess Kishna Komari, was sought in marriage by three powerful suitors. She could not wed all three, and her father feared the vengeance of the fierce men who quarrelled over his daughter's hand. Lest their savage disputes might end in attack upon his city and palace, he said that his daughter must die. "She took the poison offered her, smiling, saying to her weeping mother, 'Why grieve? A Rajput maiden often enters the world but to be sent from it. Rather thank my father for giving you me till to-day.'"

CHAPTER III

IN THE LAND OF THE RAJPUTS (*continued*)

THE ancient town of Chitore still stands on its ridge, with its grey lines of ruined walls and towers broken by two beautiful Towers of Victory, which raise their slender columns toward the sky. The smaller tower is very old, having been raised in A.D. 896, and the larger was built in A.D. 1439 to celebrate a victory of the Rajputs over their Moslem enemies. The latter is ornamented with most beautiful carving, rises to the height of 130 feet, and is divided into nine stories.

Some sixty miles from Chitore lies Oudeypor, or Udaipur, a Rajput city of great fame, for it is said to be the most beautiful city in all India. It is also of deep interest as being one of the few cities where the old native life goes on almost untouched by the presence and influence of the white people in the land. Here strut Rajput nobles in silken robes decked with gems, and followed by splendidly clothed and armed retainers. Here the elephant is seen at its proper work of carrying stately howdahs, carved and gilded and hung about with curtains of rich brocade, while long flowing draperies of cloth of gold, embroidered in the most lovely patterns and in the most striking and brilliant colours, sweep down the broad flanks of the huge slow-moving beast, and almost brush the ground with long fringed tassels. Here are bevies of women who resemble a moving garden in their shining silks of every hue that is soft and delicate, and here are naked coolies, whose bronze bodies glisten with sweat as they toil along under their load of water-skins or huge baskets heaped with earth.

The people in the streets of Udaipur strike the traveller at once as a finer type than usual. The men are tall, slender, and of lofty bearing; their features are fine, sharp, and regular. As regards the women's features you cannot judge, for in Udaipur the rule that no woman's face shall be seen by a stranger is very strictly observed. Even the poorest woman, however busily she may be at work, has a hand at liberty to draw her filmy veil of coloured gauze, red or green or blue or pink, across her face when anyone glances her way.

As the crowd passes along, two things above all strike our eyes—the beards of the men, the jewellery of the women. The beard of the Rajput is very black; it is combed and brushed till it shines in the sun; it is as large as he can grow it; then it is parted in the middle, and drawn round the face so that it stands out on either side, and the ends are curled. It is said that a Rajput dandy who cannot get his beard to properly part in the middle will draw it round his face to the required shape, and then tie a bandage tightly round his head to train the hair to the mode which he and his friends affect.

The jewellery of the women is overwhelming, and this word is meant in its literal sense: the women are absolutely loaded with ornaments. If they are wealthy, the ornaments are of gold, decked with precious stones; the poorer classes are weighed down with silver. A Rajput woman often carries on her person the wealth of her house, and may be regarded as the family savings bank. One writer, speaking of the ornaments upon a working woman of the lower classes, says:

"Her smaller toes were decked with rings of silver, made by an ingenious arrangement of small movable knobs set close together. She wore a bracelet of the same design, which was one of the most artistic and effective triumphs of the jeweller's art that I have ever seen. Upon her eight fingers she wore twenty-six rings. She carried on her left lower arm a row of many bracelets, mainly of silver, but with here and there a band of lacquer, either green or red or yellow. Upon her left upper arm she displayed a circlet of links carved into the shape of musk-melons, each the size of a nutmeg. From this fell three chains, each five inches long, and terminated with a tassel of silver. Upon her right arm she had also many bracelets. Finally, upon her neck was a chain of silver, of such length that, after it had been coiled several times round her throat, sufficient remained to fall in a double loop upon her bosom, where a heart-shaped silver charm finished both it and her scheme of display."

Another writer gives a sketch of a Rajput dandy which forms a good companion picture to the above: "A long-skirted tunic or frock of white muslin, close-fitting white trousers, and a rose-coloured turban with a broad band of gold lace and tall flashing plume of dark heron feathers and gold filigree were the salient points. Other accessories were the sword-belt, crossing his breast and encircling his waist, of dark green velvet, richly worked with pure gold, and thickly studded with emeralds, rubies, and brilliants ; a transparent yellow shield of rhinoceros hide, with knobs of black-and-gold enamel ; a sash of stiff gold lace, with a crimson thread running through the gold ; bracelets of the dainty workmanship known as Jeypore enamel, thickly jewelled, which he wore on his wrists and arms ; and there were strings of dull, uncut stones about his neck. The skirts of his tunic were pleated with many folds and stood stiffly out, and when he mounted his horse a servant on each side held them so that they might not be crushed.

"The trappings of the horse were scarcely less elaborate. His neck was covered on one side with silver plates, and his mane, which hung on the other side, was braided, and lengthened by black fringes, relieved by silver ornaments. White yaks' tails hung from beneath the embroidered saddle-cover on both sides, and his head, encased in a headstall of white enamelled leather and silver, topped with tall aigrettes, was tied down by an embroidered scarf to give his neck the requisite curve."

The streets through which these gay figures move are worthy of them. Hardly two houses are alike, but all are beautiful in "this shining white pearl among cities." No building is bare. Its front is decorated with half-columns, carved panels, or frescoes in brilliant colours, picturing horses, elephants, and tigers in pursuit of their prey. Balconies and projecting windows are faced with panels of stonework so delicately carved and fretted as to resemble lacework, and in the most beautiful and graceful patterns. And everything is white, glittering white, under a clear, glowing sky, and set beside a great lake as blue as a great sheet of turquoise.

Along the streets flows a most mingled crowd, clad in all the hues of the rainbow, and through this brilliant throng all kinds of beasts of burden thread their way. The mighty elephant, rolling along with his ponderous tread, is followed by a tiny ass no bigger than a large dog. Oxen just as small as the asses, and long-legged camels with great loads on their humped backs, come and go, and people on balconies lean over the parapets and gaze idly on the busy scene.

The most striking thing in Udaipur is the vast palace of the native Prince. The most beautiful things are the two lovely water palaces which stand on islands in the lake.

The former is entered by a fine triple-arched gateway. "Above this gateway soars the great white fabric, airy, unreal, and fantastic as a dream, stretching away in a seemingly endless prospective of latticed cupolas, domes, turrets, and jutting oriel windows, rising tier above tier, at a dizzy height from the ground. A single date-tree spreads its branches above the walls of the topmost court, at the very apex of the pile."

From the foot of the ridge on which stands this glittering pile of splendid masonry the dark blue lake stretches away, its surface broken by two islands, each of which is occupied by a water palace of wonderful beauty. Here one may roam through miles of courts, saloons, corridors, pavilions, balconies, terraces, a fairyland of splendour, in which every room, every gallery is decorated with the most exquisite art. And all this has been wrought by the hand of man, not merely the marvellous palaces, but the very lake itself. This site was once a desert valley, but immense wealth and boundless power have filled the great hollow with blue water, and littered its shores with temples and palaces and pavilions, presenting a scene which, for charm of colour and beauty of outline, can nowhere be surpassed.

CHAPTER IV

IN THE PUNJAB

Beyond the wide desert which stretches along the north-western border of Rajputana lie the plains of the Punjab, running up to the foot-hills of the Himalayas. The Punjab (the Land of Five Rivers), where the Indus and its tributaries roll their waters to the Arabian Sea, is, above all and beyond all, the battlefield of India. For it was upon these plains that the onsets of invaders first fell. Greeks, Persians, Afghans—swarm after swarm poured through the only vulnerable point of Northern India, and fought out on the plains

A SIKH WARRIOR. *Page 11*

of the Punjab the struggles which meant for them victory or disastrous retreat.

The last native rulers of the Punjab were the finest ones of all—the Sikhs. The Sikhs, a nation of fanatics and heroes, fought the Moslems for hundreds of years, and the prize was the rule of the Punjab. The Sikhs won, and formed a barrier behind which India was safe from the savage Moslem tribes of the north-west.

The Sikhs are a warrior race pure and simple. They make splendid soldiers under white officers, and the fine Sikh regiments are the pride of our native Indian army. They did not yield up the Punjab to British rule without a stern struggle. They were noble foes, and they proved noble friends. They accepted the British Raj once and for all. Within ten years after their conquest the Indian Mutiny broke out. The Sikhs stood firm, and aided the British with the utmost gallantry and devotion.

The Sikh is a fine, tall, upstanding fellow, with an immense beard and a huge coil of hair. This follows on his belief that it is impious either to shave or to cut the hair. He holds tobacco in abhorrence, and worships his Bible, which is called the Granth. In every Sikh temple sits a priest reading in a loud voice from the Granth, while beside him an attendant priest fans the holy book with a gilt-handled plume of feathers.

The most famous Sikh temple is at Amritsar, the holy city of the Sikh faith. Here is the Pool of Immortality, and in the midst of the lake rises the

Golden Temple, standing on an island. From the gates of the city a throng of stalwart, bearded Sikh pilgrims sets always towards the Golden Temple. You follow in their train, and come suddenly upon a wide open space. It is bordered by a marble pavement, and within the pavement lies the famous Lake of Immortality. The Golden Temple rises before you, glittering with blinding radiance in the hot sunshine, and mirrored in the smooth water which runs to the foot of its walls.

But you may not yet enter the sacred place and walk round the lake and see the temple. At the gates you are stopped, and your boots taken from you, and silken slippers tied on in their place. If you have tobacco in your pockets that, too, must be handed over, and left till you return, for tobacco would defile the holy place. Then you are led round by a Sikh policeman, who will show you the temple and the hallowed ground.

The marble pavement around the sacred lake is dotted with groups of priests and pilgrims, and behind the pavement stand palaces of marble, owned by great Sikh chiefs who come here to worship. Here and there are flower-sellers weaving long chains of roses and yellow jasmine to sell to worshippers who wish to make offerings. A teacher with a little band of students around him is seated beside the pool, and in a shady corner is a native craftsman busy fashioning wooden spoons and combs, and other trifles, which he sells as souvenirs of the shrine.

The Golden Temple itself is gained by a causeway

across the lake, and the causeway is entered through a magnificent portal with doors of silver, and four open doors of chased silver give access to the sanctuary itself. Here sits the high-priest reading the Granth, and before the holy book is spread a cloth, upon which the faithful lay offerings of coins or flowers.

From Amritsar, the holy city, to Lahore, the capital of the Punjab, is only some thirty miles. Lahore is a large town of great importance as a military station, and many troops are quartered in the grand old fort built by the Mogul Kings. Some of the palaces which once filled this ancient fortress still show traces of their former splendour. There are sheets of striking tilework, with panels of elephants, horsemen, and warriors worked in yellow upon a blue ground. There are marble walls inlaid most beautifully with flowers formed of precious stones. But many of the halls have been converted into barracks, and in spots where once an Emperor smoked his jewelled "hubble-bubble," surrounded by a glittering Court, Tommy Atkins, in khaki and putties, with his helmet on the back of his head, now puffs calmly at a clay pipe.

Lahore has streets which display some of the finest wood-carving in India. These streets lie within the city, the old part of the town, enclosed by brick walls sixteen feet high, and entered by thirteen gates. In one street every house has a balcony or jutting window of old woodwork, carved into the most beautiful or fantastic designs, according to the fancy of the owner who built and designed it long ago. The balconies are of all sizes and shapes, and their line is delightfully irregular. The walls, too, are painted and decorated lavishly, and domed windows are adorned by gaily-tinted peacocks worked in wood or stucco. The splendid woodwork, the shining beauty of paint and courses of bricks richly glazed in red and blue, the gay crowd which throngs the way—all these things combine to form a striking and splendid picture.

At the end of this marvellous street rise the tall minarets of the Great Mosque, and close by is the fine tomb where lies Runjit Singh, the greatest of the Sikh rulers. Under him the Sikhs rose to the height of power in India; but a few years after his death, in 1839, the Punjab passed into our hands.

CHAPTER V

AMONG THE HIMALAYAS

INDIA is bounded and guarded on the north by one of the grandest mountain-chains in the world. This is the mighty range of the Himalayas, which stretches a row of lofty peaks from east to west, as if to shut up India behind a gigantic wall.

There are very few points where this vast range can be crossed, and then only with the greatest difficulty. The most famous pass of all lies in the north-west, the well-known Khyber or Khaibar Pass leading into Afghanistan. Through this pass invader after invader in age after age has poured his troops into the fertile plains of Hindostan.

At this point Alexander the Great at the head of a Greek army crossed the Indus and marched into India. To this day there are left in the land tokens of that far-off raid. The Indian hakims, the native doctors, practise the Greek system of medicine, and the influence of the invaders is seen in old Indian coins which turn up with Greek inscriptions upon them, in statues which are found in the soil, as full of Greek feeling as any in Athens itself.

But it is now a task for British brains and hands to see to it that no fresh invader swoops through the pass, and it is very strictly guarded. In itself the pass presents many difficulties. The way lies through tremendous ravines, beside which tower precipices of stupendous height, and the road could easily be blocked and destroyed at many points. The people who inhabit this region are also of a very savage and dangerous character. They are called Afridis, and belong to wild hill-tribes, who are always ready for a fray, all the more so if there is a little plunder to be gained by it.

With these fierce and lawless people the British officers have come to an arrangement: that for two days a week the Afridis themselves shall furnish soldiers to guard the pass. For this duty an annual payment is made, and thus the Khaibar Pass is quite safe on Tuesdays and Fridays. On other days the traveller must look out for himself. He must keep a wide eye open for the Zakka Khels, a notorious Afridi tribe. When a son is born to a Zakka Khel woman she swings him over a hole in a wall, saying, "Be a thief! be a thief!" And a thief he is to the end of his days.

Among the Himalayas to the north-east of the Khyber Pass lies the beautiful vale of Kashmir, or Cashmere (the Happy Valley). Cashmere is a lofty plain, yet it is not a plateau, for you go down into it from every side. It is so high that its climate is nearer to that of England than any other part of India. The summer is like a fine English summer, but a little hotter, and with more settled weather. In winter the snow lies on the ground for two or three months, but about the end of February the snow disappears, and the spring bursts out, and the vale becomes beautiful with the tender green of growing crops and grass and a profusion of most lovely flowers. The scenery is very fine. Around and far off is the great wall of lofty mountains, which encompass the plain with glittering slopes of eternal snow. The vale itself is dotted with hamlets and villages, with fields waving with corn and rice, with meadows, with orchards of mulberry- and walnut-trees, with forests of giant plane-trees.

The capital is Srinagar, the City of Sun, whose many waterways winding through the ancient city make it an Asiatic Venice. "The houses on the banks are of many stories, most of them richly ornamented with carved wood, while the sloping roofs of nearly all are overgrown with verdure. The dome of one Hindoo temple was covered with long grass thickly studded with scarlet poppies and yellow mustard. On all sides are to be seen the remains of ancient temples and palaces, testifying to what a magnificent city Srinagar must have been."

Moving east along the Himalayan slopes, the next point of interest is the small town of Simla. This is important, not in itself, but as the seat of government in the summer, when the Viceroy and his staff escape to its cool heights from the burning plain 7,000 feet below. "By the time the month of May is advancing the season for Simla has begun. The Viceroy and his Government, with some of the official classes, have arrived, and the world of Anglo-Indian fashion have assembled. Social gatherings on the greensward underneath the rocks, overshadowed by the fir, pine, and cedar, are of daily occurrence. The rich bloom of the rhododendrons lends gorgeousness to the scene.

"The place is like a gay Swiss city isolated on the mountain-top, with dark ilex forests around it, blue hills beyond, and the horizon ever whitened by the Snowy Range. But in this paradise, tempting the mind to banish care and forget affairs of State, the most arduous business is daily conducted. Red-liveried messengers are running to and fro all the day and half the night. Tons of letters and dispatches come and go daily. Here are gathered up the threads of an Empire. Hence issue the orders affecting perhaps one-sixth of the human race."

In winter Simla is deserted. The Viceroy and his staff, the gay world of fashion, all have gone back to the plains, and in severe weather the little town often lies deep in snow.

Simla lies near the Siwalik Hills, one of the many foot-ranges which lead up to the greater heights of the Himalayas, and the Siwalik Hills are famous, because through them the sacred Ganges bursts out upon the plains of Hindostan. It is at the city of Hardwar that the Ganges forces its bright blue stream through a wild gorge and leaves the mountains for ever; and Hardwar is a holy place. The city lies in the gorge beside the stream. It has one principal street running along the river; the others mount the hill-side as steeply as staircases. Temples and ghats line the bank, and hither come vast numbers of pilgrims to the great annual fair of Hardwar to bathe in the holy river. At that time the country round resembles a vast encampment, "and all the races, faces, costumes, customs, and languages of the East, from Persia to Siam, from Ceylon to Siberia, are represented."

CHAPTER VI

AMONG THE HIMALAYAS (*continued*)

But to see the Himalayas in all their majesty we must still keep our faces to the east, and travel on towards the great central knot, where Mount Everest and the Kanchanjanga spring nearly 30,000 feet, about five and a half miles, towards the sky. Of these two mountain giants Mount Everest, though the highest measured mountain in the world, presents the less imposing appearance. This is because it lies so far in the interior of the range, and is surrounded by a girdle of snowy peaks which seem to gather about and protect their lord. They, however, block the way for a

THE GOLDEN TEMPLE, AMRITSAR. *Page 18.*

complete view of the enormous height, and thus seem to dwarf it.

For majestic splendour, Kanchanjanga bears away the palm. From the vale of the great Ranjit River, a huge rushing torrent which pours past its base, the whole immense mountain-slope may be surveyed in a single prospect, a most sublime and splendid view. The traveller who climbs the flanks of this great mountain will pass through belts of vegetation reminding him of every zone on the earth's surface. He begins his climb among the eternal green of tropical forests, through thickly-matted jungle where large creepers bind tree to tree, and great bunches of gaudily-coloured flowers blaze in the scorching heat of the tropical sun.

From the land of palm and plantain and orchid he ascends through groves of bamboo, of orange, and of fig until he gains a height at which the air is sensibly cooler, and the vegetation of temperate zones begins to appear. On the border between the two zones grow splendid tree-ferns, rhododendrons forty feet high, and groves of magnolia. When the two latter are in blossom the scene is gorgeous, and the white flowers of the magnolia seem to sprinkle the forests with snow.

The trees are now those familiar to English eyes: the oak, chestnut, willow, cherry, and beneath them grow the bramble, raspberry, strawberry, and other well-remembered plants and shrubs. Deep ravines score the flanks of the hills, and down each ravine dashes a brimming torrent, tossing its spray over ferns and wild-flowers, and butterflies with wings of the most striking and beautiful colours flit to and fro in the sunlight.

On goes the traveller, and now the underwood begins to thin, and the land becomes more grassy, and the trees to gather themselves into serried ranks of gigantic pines, firs, junipers, and larches. Up and up he climbs, and at last the belt of forest is left behind. He is out on the upper pastures beneath the open sky; he has gained the Alpine region of the Himalayas. Fields of flowers run upwards—of poppies, of edelweiss, of gentians—until at length the traveller stands at the foot of the first snow-field, and sees above him the vast sweeps of snowy glacier, the icy precipices and pinnacles which forbid his further advance.

We are now in the neighbourhood of the pass through which our troops marched into Tibet in the advance to Lhassa. The pass is approached from Darjiling, famous as a tea-growing centre, and Darjiling is approached by a mountain-railway. The latter is a triumph of engineering, so cleverly does it twist and turn its way among the hills, skirting the edge of deep precipices, winding round spirals, and affording splendid views at almost every turn of the way.

At the point where the railway starts for Darjiling the Himalayas spring up abruptly from the Indian plains. The first station is some 300 miles from Calcutta and the sea, yet less than 400 feet from sea-level. Then in less than 40 miles it climbs some 7,000 feet up to Darjiling.

This town is not only a great centre of the tea

industry, but is also one of the show places of the world, for it commands the grandest known landscape of snowy mountains in the Himalayas. Kanchanjanga is the chief figure in the glorious panorama of snow-clad heights, but Everest can be seen in the distance, and a whole host of minor peaks, each taller than Mont Blanc, carry the eye from point to point in the widespread survey.

At Darjiling may be seen many Tibetans with their praying-wheels, which they twist as they repeat their Buddhist prayers, and their praying-flags, long poles of bamboo from which flutter strips of cotton cloth, on which prayers are written. The bazaar is frequented by the people of the country round about, and many different types of the hill-tribes may be seen there.

"There are Tibetans who have come down over the passes through Sikkim ; Lepchas, from Sikkim itself, who look almost like Chinese, the women wearing heavy ear ornaments, and both men and women parting the hair in the middle and combing it down on either side ; Bhutras, the women some of them rather pretty, with necklaces, carrying a silver charm-case and with large ear-rings, and the men with pigtails ; Nepali women, with enormous carved necklaces, head-dresses of silver, and nose ornaments, which sometimes hang down over the chin ; and coolies carrying great loads on their backs, supported by a wicker band across the forehead."

In the valley around Darjiling the slopes of the hills are covered with tea-bushes, and the cultivation extends to the foot of the range, where great tea-plantations stretch over the Terai. The Terai is the name given to a broad strip of land lying along the base of the Himalayas. Here the tea-plant flourishes, but so does a terrible wasting fever, which makes the growing of these precious leaves a dangerous task. For the Terai is fearfully unhealthy. Down from the broad flanks of the great range rush a thousand torrents. They overflow their banks and soak the whole country until it is a huge swamp. Then there is a very heavy rainfall, amounting to 120 inches in a year, and this further saturates the sodden ground. The tropical sun beats upon this marshy land and raises a thick vapour which is laden with malaria. Those who live and work among this vapour are liable to be struck down by a wasting fever. The fever is very deadly to Europeans, nor do the natives themselves escape. The coolies who work in the tea-fields die of it in large numbers.

At one time the natives used to fire the jungle regularly. This great sweep of flame through the region did much towards purifying the air ; but firing the jungle is now forbidden, for fear of harming the tea-bushes and the houses of the planters.

The sight of a tea-plantation is curious rather than pretty. The bushes have no beauty : they stand in long, neat rows, and each bush is trimmed to keep it low, broad, and flat. From a distance a tea-garden looks like a great bed of huge cabbages. Among these bushes groups of coolies, both men and women, are very busily at work, for there is plenty to do, not merely in gathering the leaves, but in keeping the bushes free from weeds, which would check and hinder their growth. Under the burning sun and in the moist earth weeds spring up in great profusion, and a plantation neglected for even a short time becomes choked with them.

All the tea-bushes are not alike. Some are of a darker colour than the rest, and the leaves are smaller. This is the China plant, while the lighter-coloured bushes with larger leaves are the Assam strain. The coolies at work among the plants are gaunt, thin, miserable-looking figures. This is not to be wondered at when their occupation is considered, exposing them as it does to attack after attack of the terrible Terai fever. When the rains are very heavy they often have to work knee-deep in water and mud beneath a burning sun, and this reduces their strength to withstand the poisonous malaria.

When the coolies have filled their baskets with leaves, they carry them up to the tea-factory. First, the leaves are weighed, to see how much each coolie has plucked; then they are carried to the withering-house. All the leaves are spread out on shallow canvas trays, and left all night to wither. Next morning the leaves are put into the rolling-machine, and after half an hour's rolling they come out in a huge wet mass of leaf. This mass is broken up and spread out to dry on trays, and left for some time to ferment. The process of fermentation is carefully watched, for upon this the aroma of the tea will depend, and the process must be checked at the right moment.

Of all the rooms in the tea-factory the fermenting-room is the most pleasant to visit. It is filled with the most delightful fragrance. Next, the tea is thrown into a machine, where it is dried by hot air, and after that it enters a huge sieve, where the first rough division of the crop is made into large and small leaves. The next sorting is by hand, when nimble fingers swiftly pick out the finer sorts of tea. After this final separation the tea is dried once more, and then taken to the warehouse, where it is packed ready to go into the market.

CHAPTER VII

THE GREAT PLAINS OF THE GANGES

Beyond the Terai the traveller, turning his back upon the Himalayas, enters a vast plain, hundreds of miles wide and a thousand miles long. From Calcutta in the east to beyond Delhi in the north-west, from the Himalayas in the north to the Vindhya Hills in the south spreads this vast sweep of land, the Plain of Hindostan.

Into this plain flow a thousand streams, great and small, from the mountains which fringe its borders. Every stream, sooner or later, is gathered into the broad bosom of the Ganges, which winds its majestic current through the centre of the immense level. The Ganges is more than the great river of India: it is one of the great rivers of the world. To vast numbers of mankind it is a sacred stream, and to bathe in its holy waters is a privilege for which pilgrims will travel on foot from distant lands. But the mighty flood is put to other uses than that of worship. A network of canals gathers up the waters of itself and of its many tributaries, and spreads them abroad upon the fields of the husbandman, and makes the plain blossom into fertility.

To travel this plain reminds one of being at sea. On all hands it stretches away absolutely flat, and fades away into a misty horizon, save that at morning and evening the great snowy heights of the Himalayas shine out, and fade away again in the light of the rising and setting sun.

This great sunny plain swarms with life. It is covered with the villages of the Indian peasants; it is coloured with the bright patches of their crops, with green fields of paddy (rice), with golden wheat and barley, with poppies white in flower, with yellow mustard, with lentils, potatoes, castor-oil plants, and a score of other crops. These grow freely where water is. Where water is not, the land stretches bare and sterile, sand, stones, and rocks bleaching in the sun.

Here and there a group of trees proclaims a village. The palm and the feathery bamboo mingle their foliage; the huge banyan-tree stretches itself over the soil and sends down its long shoots, which strike it into the soil and form supports to the parent branches. Around the village pastures the herd of buffaloes, often watched by a small boy, and a clumsy cart, with wheels formed of two circles of solid wood, and drawn by two mild-eyed, hump-backed oxen, creaks by as it journeys towards a neighbouring place.

The life of the villages in this plain is, as a rule, untouched by modern ideas. They move upon the world-old ways which their fathers followed. In many of them, far from the main river and the railway, a white face is scarcely ever seen. There are great towns in the Ganges basin, but these are only specks on the face of the mighty plain. The Indian ryot knows nothing of them and goes on in his own way.

Water is his first need, and lucky is the man who has a good well or whose field is upon the bank of a river. The water is drawn in many ways. One peasant employs the simple method of watering by hand, filling his pots and emptying them upon the roots of the thirsty plants; but if the crop be rice, which demands a flood of water, a pair of oxen are set to the work. They are harnessed to a rope which runs over a pulley and has a huge water-skin fastened to its farther end. As the oxen go away from the well they pull up the skin full of water till it reaches a prepared channel. Here a man is waiting, who empties the skin into the channel, and the water runs away to the field. Now the oxen come back, and the skin sinks to the water; then they turn again, and the skin rises. One man drives the team, the other empties the water, and so the work goes on from dawn to dark.

These are the people who produce the wealth of India, these quiet, patient toilers growing their endless crops of wheat, of rice, of barley, of poppies for opium, of cotton, and of maize. They cut their ditches for irrigation, and flood a once-barren stretch of country with water. Thenceforth they take from it always two, and often three, crops in a year.

WATERING CATTLE Pl. 432

CHAPTER VIII

THE LAND OF THE MOGUL KINGS

FAR in the north-west of the great plain of Hindostan, the ancient and famous city of Delhi stands on the broad Jumna, the chief tributary of the Ganges, and around her lies the land of the Mogul Kings. Delhi has a great name in the history of India. She saw the empire of the powerful Mogul Kings; she saw some of the most desperate fighting of the Great Indian Mutiny of 1857, when the last Mogul was driven from his throne. But long before the Mutiny the power of the Moguls had vanished. Their palmy days were in the sixteenth and seventeenth centuries, and the strongest of them all, Akbar, the Great Mogul, began to reign in 1556. He came to the throne two years before Elizabeth became Queen of England; he died two years after her, in 1605.

Akbar the Great was only fourteen years old when he became King, but "from that moment his grip was on all India." He proved a wonderful ruler and leader of men. India was a welter of conflicting races, tongues, and creeds. Under his firm and wise government strife died away, peace and order took its place, and those who had been the fiercest enemies lived side by side in friendship. He was at once law-maker, soldier, ruler, and philosopher. He was tall, and as strong in body as in mind, for he was the best polo player in India, and it is recorded of him that he once rode 800 miles on camel-back, and then, without staying for rest, at once gave battle to his enemy.

To find the wonderful buildings which the Great Mogul left behind him, we must leave Delhi and go down the Jumna to Agra and its neighbourhood. Agra is still called by the natives Akbarabad, the city of Akbar, and here stands the mighty fort which the monarch built, a city in itself. In a land of magnificent buildings there is nothing grander than the fort at Agra. Its battlements of red sandstone tower 70 feet from the ground, the walls run a mile and a half in circuit, and the immense mass of masonry dwarfs the modern town. Within the fort is a maze of courts, pavilions, corridors, and chambers, wrought in dazzling white marble, and decorated with the most beautiful carving and exquisite tracery in stone. The chief features of the vast building are Akbar's palace, with its golden pinnacles glittering in the sunshine, and the Moti Masjid, a small mosque of most beautiful proportions, so perfect both in design and in the beauty of its ornaments that it is called the Pearl Mosque, being the pearl of all mosques.

From Agra a drive of twenty-two miles takes us to Fattehpore-Sikri, a marvellous town, erected by Akbar himself, "where every building is a palace, every palace a dream carved in red sandstone." The name of the place means "The City of Victory," and was given to it because Akbar's grandfather defeated the Rajputs at this place in 1527. Here Akbar built a splendid mosque, which stands on the west side of a great courtyard. From the south the courtyard is entered by the

Sublime Gate, or Gate of Victory, "the noblest portal in India." Akbar's palace may still be seen, and the chief place of interest is the Throne Room, where, in the centre of a large chamber, rises a huge column of red sandstone, with a spreading capital surrounded by a balustrade. Akbar's seat was placed on the top of this mighty pillar, and from it ran four raised pathways, leading to the places where his ministers sat, in four galleries, one at each corner of the room.

The tomb of Akbar is at Sikandra, about six miles from Agra. It stands in the midst of a garden, which is entered by four lofty gateways of red sandstone. From each gateway a broad causeway of stone runs to the centre of the enclosure, where rises the great building which contains the tomb of the Great Mogul. The building rises in terraces something in the form of a pyramid, the lower stories of red sandstone, the top story of white marble, the latter decorated with pierced panels of marble wrought in the most beautiful patterns. The floor of the building is open to the day, and in the centre stands the grandly simple tomb, a huge block of white marble, on which is inscribed a single word, 'Akbar.' Near at hand is a small pillar in which the famous diamond the Koh-i-noor was once set.

Splendid as were the buildings of Akbar, yet his grandson, Shah Jehan, was destined to surpass him; for Shah Jehan built the Taj Mahal, the most glorious tomb that grief ever raised in memory of love, and one of the wonders of the world. In 1629 Shah Jehan lost his wife, and he determined to raise to her memory a monument which should keep her name immortal. He employed 20,000 men for eighteen years, and the splendid building was completed in 1648, the date being inscribed upon the great gate. The most famous artists and workmen of India were gathered to this task, and the result is a palace of the most wonderful beauty and magnificence.

The Taj Mahal stands in a great garden about a mile from Agra, and is surrounded by trees and flowers and fountains: "the song of birds meets the ear, and the odour of roses and lemon-flowers sweetens the air." It is built of the purest white marble, and shines with such dazzling brilliance that to look full upon it in strong sunshine is scarcely possible. Seen by moonlight, it is a radiant vision of beauty, and the charm of its lovely form is felt to the full. The great domes seem to swim above in the silver light, the stately minarets shoot up towards the dark blue of the sky, and the scene is one of unearthly beauty.

Glorious as is this mighty building in the mass, it is just as full of beauty when examined closely and in detail. Every part is covered with the most graceful and exquisite designs, inlaid in marbles of different colours. Every wall, every arch, every portal, is ornamented and finished as if the craftsmen had been engaged upon a small precious casket instead of a corner of an immense palace tomb. One striking feature is seen in the arches of the doorways and windows. Around them run inlaid letters most beautifully shaped in black marble. These letters form verses and chapters of the Koran, the sacred book of the Moslems, and it is said that the whole of the Koran is thus inlaid in the Taj.

The heart of the building is the vault where Shah Jehan and his wife sleep together, for he was laid beside her. The tombs are formed of the purest white marble, inlaid most beautifully with designs formed of agate, cornelian, lapis-lazuli, jasper, and other precious stones, and they are surrounded by a pierced marble screen whose open tracery-work is formed of flowers carved and wrought into a thousand designs.

CHAPTER IX

THE LAND OF THE MOGUL KINGS (*continued*)

It was Shah Jehan who returned to Delhi as the seat of government of the Mogul Kings, and largely rebuilt the city. But the memories of Delhi reach far, far back before the time of the Mogul Kings; they stretch away into the dim dawn of Indian history, where the threads of truth and fable are so intermingled that the historian cannot disentangle them.

The modern Delhi stands in the midst of a plain covered with ruins—the ruins of many cities built by many Kings before the present Delhi came into being. It is a striking sight to drive from the city to the great Tower of Kutb Minar, eleven miles away to the south. The road runs through the traces of the Delhis that have been: heaps of scattered brick, a mound that was once a gateway, a broken wall that was once the corner of a fort, a tumbling tower, and a ruined dome. Through these tokens of shattered palaces and tombs of dead and forgotten Kings you pass on till the vast shaft of the Kutb rises from the plain like a lighthouse from the sea.

It is an immense tower of five stories, rising 240 feet into the air. At the base it measures about 50 feet through, but the sides taper till it is only 9 feet wide at the top. The three lower stories are of red sandstone; the two upper are faced with white marble, and the whole forms a very striking and wonderful monument.

This colossal tower preserves the name of Kutb, one of the "slave" Sultans of Delhi. Seven hundred years ago Kutb, who had been a slave, rose by his military talents, first to the position of a General, and then made himself Emperor of Delhi. He was the first of ten Moslem rulers who reigned from 1206 to 1290, and it is believed that the Kutb Minar was raised as a tower of victory. It is possible to ascend the lofty shaft by a flight of 378 steps, which winds up the interior, but "the view from the top is nothing. The country is an infinite green and brown chess-board of young corn and fallow, dead flat on every side, ugly with the complacent plainness of all rich country. Beyond the sheeny ribbon of the Jumna, north, south, east, and west, you can see only land, and land, and land—a million acres with nothing on them to see except the wealth of India and the secret of the greatness of India."

But near at hand is a far more ancient monument

than that of the slave King. This is the famous Iron Pillar, the "arm or weapon of victory." It is a pillar of pure malleable iron, and its erection is ascribed to the fourth century before Christ, when it was raised to commemorate a great Hindu victory. At present it projects some 23 feet from the earth, and it is about a foot in diameter at the capital, but a great part of it is buried.

In Delhi itself stand the great fort and the great mosque, the Jama Masjid, both built by Shah Jehan. The fort was at once the stronghold and the palace of the Mogul Emperors who followed Shah Jehan. It is surrounded by a towering wall built of gigantic slabs of sandstone, crested with battlements and moated below. The usual entrance to the fort is through the noble Lahore Gate, and the palace stands before you.

You enter the hall of audience, a great hall of red sandstone open on three sides. There is an alcove in the centre of the wall at the back, and from the alcove projects a great slab of marble. From the four corners of this marble platform spring four richly-inlaid marble pillars supporting an arched canopy. The marble is beautiful, but the work upon it is ten times more beautiful. The wall of the alcove is gorgeous with tiny pictures of flowers and fruits and birds, wrought most cunningly in paint and precious stones. In this alcove was sometimes set the Peacock Throne, whose glories are still celebrated in story and song, the marvellous throne which Shah Jehan had built for himself, the throne which blazed with gems set by the most skilful jewellers of Delhi, men famous throughout India for their craftsmanship.

Next comes the hall of private audience, where the King sat among his Court. This, too, is open, a noble pavilion on columns, where the breezes could blow if any such were moving in the burning heats of summer. "The whole is of white marble, asheen in the sun; but that is the least part of the wonder. Walls and ceilings, pillars, and many-pointed arches, are all inlaid with richest, yet most delicate, colour. Gold cornices and scrolls and lattices frame traceries of mauve and pale green and soft azure. What must it have been, you ask yourself, when the Peacock Throne blazed with emerald and sapphire, diamond and ruby, from the now empty pedestal, and the plates of burnished silver reflected its glory from the roof?"

Peacock Throne and plates of silver have long been gone. Nadir Shah carried them off in 1739, when he entered the city with his victorious troops, put the inhabitants to the sword, and sacked the place. Many an attack has been made on the fort, but none, in English eyes, has so deep an interest as the assault of 1857, and all English travellers visit the Cashmere Gate.

The Siege of Delhi by our troops is one of the great incidents of the Indian Mutiny, and the historic ridge to the north-west is the site of the British camp. After a patient siege the fort was attacked, the Cashmere Gate was blown open by a storming-party, and the British poured in, victorious at last. Upon the gate is an inscription telling of the deeds of the noble forlorn hope who led the way and opened a path

THE TAJ MAHAL. *Page [illegible]*

for their comrades to rush in. Other monuments speak of the heroic telegraph operators who "saved India" by sending far and wide news of the Mutiny, and stuck to their posts though it cost their lives; and of the gallant party under Lieutenant Willoughby who blew up the powder-magazine in which they were posted rather than let its precious contents fall into the hands of the rebels.

Beyond the fort stands the Jama Masjid, the vast mosque, said to be the largest in the world. It is a great building of red sandstone and marble, "upstanding from a platform reached on three sides by flights of steps so tall, so majestically wide, that they are like a stone mountain." At the head of each flight is a splendid gateway, and that which faces eastward is opened for none save the Viceroy, who rules India, and the Lieutenant-Governor of the Punjab. At the mosque are preserved some Moslem relics, which the guardian priest will show for a fee—a slipper of Mohammed, a hair of the Prophet, his footprints in stone, and a piece of the green canopy which was once over his tomb.

Now we will go into the city proper. Here is indeed a change! Mill chimneys pour into the blue sky their long trails of black smoke. Marble halls and mighty Kings seem very far off as you traverse a cotton-spinning quarter where Delhi measures itself against Manchester. The narrow streets are dirty and squalid, and filled with a crowd whose dingy robes and shabby turbans bespeak the modern artisan of industrial India. Many strange things has this ancient city seen, but nothing stranger than this last turn of her fortunes, when she bends to her clacking loom, and boasts that with her own cotton she can spin as fine as any mill in Lancashire.

CHAPTER X

IN THE MUTINY COUNTRY

Now we will leave Delhi and the Jumna, and strike away to the south-east towards the parent river, the Ganges. Our journey lies across a rich portion of the Great Plain, and this portion has a name of its own. It is called the Doab, or Douab, the Land of Two Rivers, since it lies between the Jumna and the Ganges. It is a most fertile stretch of country, well watered and well tilled, yielding great crops of sugar, rice, and indigo.

At last we reach Cawnpore, on the Ganges, and now we are in the very heart of the Mutiny country. Here took place the most dreadful incident of that great struggle—the massacre of white women and children who fell into the hands of Nana Sahib, a rebel leader. Their bodies were flung into a well, and to-day a beautiful monument stands over the place. The well is enclosed by a fine stone screen, and over the gateway is carved the words: "These are they which came out of great tribulation." In the centre of the enclosure, directly over the well itself, rises the figure of a beautiful white marble angel, and the well bears this inscription: "Sacred to the perpetual memory of a great company of Christian people, chiefly women and children, who near this spot were cruelly murdered by the followers of the rebel Nana Dhundu Pant, of Bithur, and cast, the dying with the dead, into the well below, on the 15th day of July, MDCCCLVII." Near by is the pretty little cemetery where the victims were buried when the British troops seized Cawnpore two short days after the massacre.

The Cawnpore of to-day is a busy industrial town noted for the manufactures of cotton and leather, and when the visitor has seen the places connected with the massacre, the railway will soon carry him to Lucknow, where the most deeply interesting memento of the Mutiny is to be found. This is the Residency, the great house where the tiny British garrison, with hundreds of women and children in their charge, held at bay vast numbers of rebels from May to November, 1857.

The defence of Lucknow is among the finest stories of British valour and British endurance. Assault after assault was made by hordes of well-armed and well-trained mutineers, for the men who wished to slay the British had been drilled by them. Ceaseless showers of shot and shell were poured into the place, and by the middle of September two-thirds of the gallant defenders were dead of wounds or disease. Still the brave remnant held their own, and kept the foe at bay. Among the earliest losses was the greatest of all. This was the death of Sir Henry Lawrence, who governed at Lucknow. By the foresight and prudence of this great and unselfish man means were provided by which the garrison was enabled to make good its defence; but he was killed by a shell, and died on the 4th of July, 1857. His grave is covered by a marble slab, on which is carved this fine and simple inscription, chosen by himself: "Here lies Henry Lawrence, who tried to do his duty."

Towards the end of September General Havelock cut his way into Lucknow, but he had not men enough to carry away the besieged in safety. The rebels closed round the Residency once more, and the siege went on. In November Sir Colin Campbell arrived with a stronger army, and, after most desperate fighting, defeated the mutineers and relieved the heroic garrison.

As a memento of that stern struggle and noble defence, the Residency has been preserved to this day just as it stood at the end of that terrible six months. The walls still bear the marks of shot and shell, the shattered gates show where assault after assault was delivered, the brick gateway of the Baillie Guard is pointed out as the famous spot where rescued and rescuers met.

The modern city of Lucknow is one of the largest in India. Standing on the Gumti, a tributary of the Ganges, it is a place of great trade, and its large native quarter is packed with bazaars devoted to commerce. This part of the city was once famous for the excellence of its steel weapons and the beauty of its jewellers' work. But the native Princes and noblemen who purchased arms and ornaments are no longer to be found, and these arts have decayed.

In the Mutiny Country

Lucknow is the chief town in the province of Oudh, and when there were Kings of Oudh, Lucknow was their capital. The palaces of the Kings still stand in the court suburb, but there is nothing here to compare with the magnificence of Delhi or Agra. The European quarter is of great importance. Broad, smooth roads run through it, shaded by trees and bordered by turf. On either side of these pleasant roads stand the large, handsome bungalows of merchants, of officials, and of the officers in command of the strong force of troops always stationed in the place. There are beautiful gardens and parks, and the business streets are lined with handsome shops and offices.

Returning to the Ganges, and descending the course of that great stream, the next place of importance is Allahabad, standing at the point where the mighty Jumna joins its flood to the parent river. Allahabad is a town of Akbar's founding, and the Great Mogul built the fine red stone fort which is the chief object in the place. The fort looks across the broad waters of the Jumna, here about three-quarters of a mile wide. "The appearance of the Jumna, even in the dry season, strikes one as very imposing, with its enormous span from shore to shore, shut in by high, shelving, sandy banks, its then placid waters a clear bright blue. What must be the effect in the freshes, when its surging waters rush resistlessly past, and its banks are hidden by a suddenly formed expanse of water more resembling sea than river?"

The spot where the Jumna pours its bright flood into the muddy stream of the Ganges is a sacred one in the eyes of all Hindoos. Great numbers of pilgrims resort to it, above all at the time of the melas, or religious fairs, held every year at the full moon in January and February. They gather upon the sandy shores and recite their prayers and bathe in the holy river.

But there is one spot on the Ganges still more sacred to Hindoo worshippers, and that is Benares, the holy city. It lies below Allahabad, and in the fort of the latter city the mouth of a small subterranean passage is pointed out. The priests say, and the natives believe, that this passage runs to Benares.

CHAPTER XI

THE SACRED CITY OF THE HINDOOS

THERE is one city of India to which pilgrims are for ever going or returning. Its temples are always crowded with worshippers; its broad stone ghats running down to the sacred Ganges are packed day after day with adoring and reverent throngs. This is Benares, the most sacred city in the world in Hindoo eyes.

Its sacred character arises from the fact that here stands the temple of Buddha, the great Hindoo teacher, who was born six centuries before Christ, and whose followers are to be counted in myriads in India. From all parts of that great country they come on pilgrimage to see the place where their master taught, and to bathe their bodies in the sacred stream.

It is a wonderful sight to see the row of riverside palaces, temples, and ghats which here fringe the broad river. It is still more wonderful to see the vast crowd of worshippers who throng the wide stone stairs as they stream up and down to the river to make their ablutions and to repeat their prayers.

The best time to see this striking sight is at sunrise. Then the crowds are thickest, for all wish to enter the water at that instant when the sun springs into the cloudless Indian sky and pours a flood of golden splendour over the wide stream, and lights up the long row of temples and palaces which face him as he rises.

Viewed from a boat on the river, the scene is one of wonderful animation and of most brilliant colour. The broad stone steps come down the bank in stately sweep and vanish into the stream. They run on down to the river-bed, and the saying goes among the natives that the river is here so deep that it would cover the back of one elephant standing on the top of another. Each ghat is crowded with Hindoo worshippers, and their robes of bright and delicate colours make the flight of stairs look like a huge bed of flowers. But it is a bed where the flowers are on the move, and mingle with each other to form new pictures at every moment, ever-changing combinations of the most delicate pinks, blues, greens, yellows, of silk and muslin, with snowy turbans and white robes intermingled with the brighter shades.

At the foot of the great flight many worshippers are already in the water. The men cast aside their robes, and the sunlight strikes upon their brown bodies and makes them glitter like figures cast in bronze, and then flashes brighter still as the bronze glistens with the sacred water flung by the hands or poured from a brazen ewer ; the women slip a bathing-robe over their shoulders, and then remove their ordinary dress, and not only bathe themselves but their garments also in the sacred water. Many of the devotees throw offerings of sandal-wood, betel, sweet-meats, and flowers into the stream, and some of them have great garlands of flowers round their necks. These have been worshipping at a temple which gives such garlands to those who frequent it, and now these worshippers go into the stream and bend lower and lower until the garlands are raised by the water from their necks and float away down the river.

At one place clouds of smoke rise into the air, and huge fires are burning fiercely. This is the burning ghat, where the dead bodies of Hindoos are burned, and their ashes cast into the sacred Ganges. Every Hindoo wishes for this, but only the rich can have their bodies carried to Benares; for the poor it is impossible. Yet, if the poor Hindoo has a faithful friend who is going on pilgrimage, this may, in some degree, be accomplished. A frequent sight is that of a man earnestly pouring into the water a stream of ashes from a brazen vessel. The ashes are those of a friend who has died far from the sacred river, and have perhaps been brought many hundreds of miles by the pilgrim.

And so our boat might move along the stream past ghat after ghat and temple after temple, the steps packed

BENARES. *Page 46.*

with those who wish to bathe and those who have bathed. The latter spread out their clothes to dry in the sun, and sit near them, reciting prayers or reading sacred books or in the perfect silence of deep meditation, their bodies rigid and unmoving as figures cast in bronze. For miles this wonderful scene of devotion stretches along the river, and the bank is crowned with a broken line of minarets, domes, and towers, which rise against the deep blue of the sky.

The first thing for a pilgrim to do is to bathe. After that he must make the round of the city—a walk of about ten miles—and pay a visit to the temples. The ten-mile walk is more easily done than the latter task, so innumerable are the temples of the sacred place. Some, of course, are more famous than others, and every one goes to see the Monkey Temple, where offerings are made to a concourse of chattering monkeys; and the holy Golden Temple, whose dome is plated with gold, and whose shrine is always crowded with devotees. Near by is the Well of Knowledge, where the god Shiva is said to live, and this well is half filled with flowers thrown in as offerings to the god.

For twenty-five centuries Benares has been a holy city. Through this vast stretch of time an unceasing throng of pilgrims has swept to it across the great plain in which it lies. They bathe in the Ganges, and visit the temples. Then they depart for their distant homes, satisfied that they have set their eyes on the sacred places of their faith, and in sweep fresh thousands to take the place of each departing band.

CHAPTER XII

THE CAPITAL OF INDIA

Below Benares the great river flows quietly on, ever widening as its tributaries flow in on either bank, and watering as it goes vast stretches of paddy-fields. Many pilgrims from the sacred city descend it by boat as far as Patna, where they branch away to the south on a new pilgrimage. They walk some ninety miles to Buddh Gaya, where Gautama sat in deep meditation beneath the sacred Bo-tree, and became the Buddha.

The place is held in the deepest veneration by the countless followers of the Buddhist faith, and vast numbers come to this day to see and worship at the temple built upon the spot. Behind the temple still stands a pipal or Bo-tree, and the natives hold that this is the very tree beneath which the great teacher sat.

As the Ganges approaches the sea through the plains of Bengal it is joined by the mighty Brahmaputra, which has swept round the eastern end of the Himalayas, and brought the waters of Tibet down to the bay. And now the mighty stream begins to break up. The broad flood becomes diverted to innumerable channels, and flows through an immense delta to the sea. This delta is the huge, swampy flat of the Sunderbunds. The Sunderbunds are very low, very unhealthy (for the swamps breed malaria), and matted with tropical jungle. The tide flows in and the rivers flow out, making an inextricable confusion of channels, creeks, canals, waterways, of every shape, size, and direction. The water seems to flow every way at once. The traveller is perhaps being rowed up a channel, and his men are straining at the oars against a strong current. Suddenly, without change of direction, the boat is swept forward on a favouring stream. From some side creek a fresh current has poured in unnoticed, and now bears the boat on.

In times of flood or high tide the low, muddy banks can no longer hold the streams, and the whole country becomes a vast swamp. The damp soil is hidden beneath masses of canes and reed and low-growing palms, and when the feathery fronds cover the scene with a carpet of beautiful green the prospect is very lovely. Among the brakes of this thick jungle wild animals swarm in great numbers. Deer and wild-boars abound, and the broad round marks of a tiger's pads are often seen in the mud near a drinking-place. Enormous crocodiles haunt the pools and channels. From the deck of a river-steamer these huge reptiles may often be seen sunning themselves on a warm mud-bank. As the steamer draws near they glide down the bank and vanish into the water. Between their footprints a long, deep groove is left in the mud. This is made by the great tail.

The chief branch of the Ganges is the River Hughli, upon which stands Calcutta, the capital of India. Calcutta is not the capital of India because either of its beauty or position, but because of its immense trade. It is the natural outlet for the riches of the vast plains of the Ganges. Through it pour the vast stores of corn, of rice, of jute, of tobacco, of tea, of a score of other things produced by those fertile levels.

As regards position, the site of Calcutta is bad, for it lies on the flat beside the river, with the swamps of the Sunderbunds on every hand. The heats of summer are overpowering, and the Viceroy and his officials fly to Simla, high up among the Himalayas. But in the cold season the town is very gay and splendid. The European quarter is laid out on noble lines. The streets are of great width with park-like gardens, called compounds, on either side. In these compounds, filled with flowers and trees, stand large and stately mansions, princely residences such as befit the rulers of India.

The centre of Calcutta is the Maidan, or Park, a great open space beside the broad river. On its western side stands Fort William, the building of which was commenced by Clive in 1757. The original Fort William, where stood the famous "Black Hole of Calcutta," was farther to the north, and the site of the dungeon is marked in the roadway. A tablet on a wall near at hand reads: "The stone pavement close to this marks the position and size of the prison-cell in Old Fort William known in history as the Black Hole of Calcutta."

At one end of the Maidan stands the stately Government House, where the Viceroy of India dwells, and near it are many fine public buildings. The great park is bounded by the splendid streets in which are found the mansions of the European merchants, bankers, and officials, and the Maidan is the scene of the fashionable evening drive.

North of the Maidan lies the native quarter, covering six square miles, and packed with more than half a million people. The streets are narrow, and the buildings are of no great interest. The bazaars are worthy of the traveller's attention, not because they differ from bazaars elsewhere, but because of the varied crowds of a vast variety of tribes and nations which pour through this great centre of commerce.

CHAPTER XIII

ACROSS THE DECCAN

THE southern part of India is shaped like a huge triangle, and within its coasts lies a vast triangular plateau, the Deccan. In the fierce heats of summer this huge tableland lies flat and grey beneath the burning sun, save where there is water. Then village after village of tiny huts thatched with palm-leaves cluster along the banks of river or lake, and the water is lifted by every kind of ancient device and poured over the thirsty land.

Water is all this rich soil needs. Given enough of the precious fluid, the soil covers itself thickly with crops of cotton, tobacco, rice, millet, saffron, and castor-oil plant. Everywhere the land swarms with oxen, a sure sign of the people's wealth.

We are now in the territory of Hyderabad, the

greatest native State in India, ruled over by the Nizam, the chief native Prince. This capital city lies towards the south of the State, and is one of the most interesting cities in India, not so much for its beauty or its buildings, but for its life and, above all, for its military population. Hyderabad is the paradise of irregular troops, and it is also rich in regulars. Of the latter there are some thousands of British troops, and 30,000 who serve the Nizam himself; of irregulars, no man knows the number, for every noble and chief maintains a private army of his own, just as our barons did in feudal times.

It follows, then, that the streets of Hyderabad bear the appearance of a military camp. Every other man is armed to the teeth, and scarcely two alike in weapons or uniform. A figure in turban and embroidered robes, a girdle full of daggers, and a six-foot-long jezail over his shoulder, is followed by a man in trim khaki, and the latter by a trooper in burnished breastplate and helmet of polished steel. A lancer with long spear swinging from his arm jogs by, and the next horseman carries a great scimitar; and so the medley of figures and weapons passes by—rifles and matchlocks, bayonets and tulwars, chain-mail and shields of hide.

But among the swarms of irregulars, the Arab troops stand out by themselves. The Nizams are Moslem rulers, and to provide themselves with Moslem troops have done much recruiting in Arabia. The desert warriors with their rough, stern, dark features, their spare, stalwart frames, their robes of snowy white, their triple row of daggers across their bodies, look very different from the gaily-dressed, olive-faced, handsome soldiery who are native-born. The Arabs are as stern and rough as they look. More than once they have got out of hand, and it has been a question whether the Nizam ruled them or they the Nizam.

To the south-east of Hyderabad the province of Madras stretches along the shore of the Bay of Bengal. This province is famous in the history of British India. It saw the struggles between the English and the French for the mastery of the land; it saw the victories of Clive which raised him to power; it saw the rise of English authority. The chief town is Madras, a large but not a striking city, especially when seen from the sea. As the traveller approaches by steamer he sees a lofty lighthouse, a few spires, rows of tall offices and public buildings, and Fort St. George—nothing more. His vessel does not enter a bay, but a roadstead; for Madras lies upon an open stretch of coast which is at times swept by hurricanes of terrible fury. Yet, in spite of this situation, Madras ranks as the third port of India, and has a great trade. Some protection is now given to vessels by a couple of breakwaters forming a harbour.

The most interesting place in the city is Fort St. George, for here the East India Company first gained its footing in India in 1639. The fort was begun in the same year, and this was the first step taken in the path which led to British supremacy in India.

The native part of the city is known as Black Town, and is a dense mass of poorly-built native houses crowded along narrow streets, and thickly packed with Hindoo inhabitants. The European suburbs lie to the west of Black Town, and, as at other great centres, consist of fine mansions standing in spacious compounds.

To the south of Madras lies a country containing cities where some of the mightiest temples in India may be seen. Of these cities Trichinopoli and its great temple of Srirangam may be taken as an example. The temple of Srirangam is not merely, like the other temples of Southern India, of immense size ; it is the largest temple in India. Its enclosure measures about half a mile each way. It stands on an island in the River Cauvery to the north of Trichinopoli, and is a vast building which must have cost immense labour and a huge sum of money.

The chief features of this mighty temple are the Hall of a Thousand Pillars and the Horse Court, which forms the front of the hall. The Horse Court consists of eight pillars carved into the figures of horses, each pillar "representing a stallion standing on its hind-legs, its head supporting a bracket coming forward from the pillar, and its fore-feet resting on a monster attacked by the rider or on the shield of a foot-soldier who is assisting in the attack. The horses stand in other respects free from the pillars except at the tails, which are split, or rather doubled, so that each horse has two tails, one sculptured on each side of the pillar The horses, the figures, and the columns behind are carved from a single block of granite." So great is this temple that lofty trees flourish in its

NATIVE TROOPS *Page 9*

enclosure, and it is said that the priestly families who inhabit it number more than twenty thousand people.

In this part of India the fondness of the women for silver jewellery seems to be greater than elsewhere, if that be possible. Not only are they loaded with the usual rings, bracelets, armlets, and anklets, but they pierce the nose in three places to adorn it with trinkets. In each nostril a sort of brooch is fastened, and the centre of the nose is pierced to insert a large ring, which hangs down over the mouth. A large hole is opened in the lobe of the ear to hold a heavy ring as big as a bracelet, and in one district a great ear-lobe is considered a mark of beauty. It is said that women may be seen, the lobes of whose ears have been stretched and pulled out in such a manner that the owner can thrust her hand and wrist through the opening.

CHAPTER XIV

AT THE COURT OF A NATIVE PRINCE

An English traveller in India who enjoys the opportunity of paying a visit to the Court of a native Prince, often gets a glimpse of a life which has seen very little change for many hundreds of years. The native Prince himself may be fond of slipping off to London or Paris, where nothing marks him off from any other wealthy visitor save his dark brown skin, but at home he keeps the state of his forefathers, and the costume and customs of his Court may be just the same to-day as they were when Saxon and Norman were fighting at Senlac.

A state function at such a Court, for instance, as that of the ruler of Udaipur is a most splendid ceremony, and an English visitor of consequence will attend it in the company of the British Resident. The latter is the agent of the British Government. No native Prince is allowed to exercise the absolute power his fathers once held. At every native capital there is a residency, and here lives the man who is the real power behind the native throne, the representative of the British Raj.

The journey to the palace will be made upon elephants in howdahs carved and gilded and hung with rich curtains. On the neck of the elephant sits the driver in a bright dress, holding in his hand a short spear, ending in a hook and a shining point. When the riders are seated in the howdah, the driver urges the elephant forward with voice and spear, and guides him through the streets. An elephant procession through the streets of a native city is one of the noblest sights which can be seen or imagined. Two by two the huge, stately beasts, with their ponderous swaying stride, swing along between the rows of houses, whose gaily adorned flat tops and terraces and balconies are crowded by spectators in newly-washed robes of every colour which is bright, and fresh, and gay. Here and there in the procession float glittering standards of silk worked in gold and precious stones, and the gay dress of the drivers, the richly-decorated howdahs, the splendid draperies which almost conceal the great elephants, all shining and flashing in the sun, present a wonderful picture of beautiful and stately movement.

As the procession draws near the palace the way is guarded by native troops, and these exhibit another striking scene. Their ranks do not present the monotony of Western uniforms. Each band of the Prince's body-guard wears the dress of that part of his dominions whence it was drawn, and a bewildering variety of garbs and arms may be seen. One troop is dressed like the Saracens who fought in the Crusades. They wear armour of chain mail and glittering steel helmets, and carry lances and great curved scimitars. Next, the line is guarded by warriors in massive turbans, clothed in robes of rich stuffs, and armed with sword, spear, and shield, and with quaint firelocks slung over the shoulder. Next stand men in gleaming breastplates, whose helmets are sharply pointed, and whose girdles are stuffed with daggers and pistols. Others bear huge maces or heavy axes, and, in fine, almost every weapon with which man has ever waged war may be seen in the lines of stalwart warriors who keep the way.

At the palace itself the outer halls are filled with the nobles and chiefs who owe allegiance to the Prince. They are armed and equipped like their followers without, but in more splendid fashion. Jewels glitter and glow on great silken turbans; robes are stiff with gold and costly embroidery; girdles are heavy with weapons, whose handles are richly chased and set with diamonds and rubies; pearls and emeralds and sapphires flash from necklet or armlet.

Through these the visitors pass on to inner halls, where they are received by members of the reigning family and escorted to the hall of audience.

Here, in a noble chamber, the Prince will be seated in state on a splendid throne. On either side stand attendants, waving fans made of feathers or of horse-hair. The latter are only used to fan a Prince, and are the emblems of sovereignty.

The English guests are seated on chairs, and the nobles and chiefs, who have followed them into the room, seat themselves on the beautiful carpets spread over the floor. All except the guests are barefooted, for the native company have left their gilded slippers outside the chamber.

The Prince and his guests converse, and very often presents are given and offered—shawls, silks, brocade, or jewels. Perhaps nautch-girls will come in and dance. They wear robes of shining gauze from head to foot, and they dance with slow, graceful movements, often singing as they move.

At last the Prince calls for essence of roses with the leaf of the betel-nut, and this is the signal that the interview is over. Now the guests will be conducted over the palace, to see the public rooms and courts; but the zenana, the women's apartments, are never shown; nor is the visitor supposed even to glance towards the lattices and trellised windows, behind which the native ladies are probably having a good look at him. The evening will close with a grand illumination and display of fireworks, managed with the utmost skill. From a terrace, so placed that the dark smooth mirror of a lake lies between himself and the illuminations, the visitor looks upon a fairy scene. The pavilions, the courts, the balconies, the lines of the palace itself, will be picked out in points of fire, and the whole is mirrored in the water. Then the fireworks leap into the sky—rockets, great globes of many colours, fountains spouting golden fire, and pictures of forts outlined in flame and firing heavy broadsides from mimic cannon. Finally the visitor climbs the ladder set against the side of his elephant, while the band blares out, "God Save the King," and goes home to dream of the wonderful things he has seen, and to try to disentangle the host of pictures which dance before his eyes when he reflects upon his visit to a native Court.

CHAPTER XV

THE RELIGIOUS MENDICANTS

INDIA is the land of religious mendicants. They swarm in every part of it; they are seen moving along the country roads and in the streets of villages and towns; they flock around every shrine.

Some are simply wanderers; they have abandoned all earthly goods, have left their homes, and taken their place among the poorest. Smearing themselves with ashes, their only garment a wisp of rag—and this they wear simply because the police will not let them go without it—they ramble from holy place to holy place. "Naked, homeless, he eats only when food is offered to him, drinks only from the cup of cold water which is given in the name of the Lord."

Many of these men have been rich and powerful members of the society in which they moved. Then a day came when they laid aside their robes of muslin and silk embroidered with gold; they left their great houses filled with troops of servants; without a word they slipped away from wife, from children, from friends, and the place they had filled knew them no more. They had gone to wander far and wide through the vast plains, the mighty hills of India—strange, naked, wild-looking figures, unwashed, unshorn, looking the veriest outcasts of the earth.

Why is this done? For this reason. They feel deeply the vanity of earthly things; they believe that the more one can get rid of the needs and the wants of the body, the nearer he will get to the Divine. So they cast aside everything which pampers the body and makes this life sweet, and forsake all things of this world in favour of prayer and meditation.

It is not uncommon to meet a man who has the air of a naked, half-crazy savage, and to find that man capable of arguing in the most able manner on the highest topics. Mrs. Steel remarks: "They are often extremely well educated. They will knock a false argument into a cocked hat with easy ability. Some of them—these naked savages—will astonish you by quoting Herbert Spencer; for even nowadays they are recruited from all classes, and they belong by rights to the most thoughtful of each class." Such men as these belong, of course, to the highest order of the religious mendicants. The majority of their fellows are of a much lower order, but one and all they practise poverty and live only upon alms.

Many of them, of the fakir class, practise all kinds of self-torture upon themselves. One, perhaps, has held up his arm above his head for so many years that it is now immovable, and stands straight up from his shoulder, thin and shrunken, and as stiff as a piece of wood. Another has held his fingers close shut in his palm until the nails have grown through the flesh and stand out at the back of the hand. A third has lain for many years on a bed of spikes, until his skin, hard as horn, renders so uneasy a bed no discomfort. There are fakirs who have not stood upright once in forty years. They travel by crawling, and as their cry rings along the village street, the pious hasten to bring them a handful of rice or a cup of water. It would be useless to offer them better fare; they would refuse it. An account is given of one fakir who sat so long without moving at the foot of a tree that the roots grew around him and fettered him to his place.

Many observers have been extremely puzzled by certain powers which these fakirs possess. Fakirs have been seen to walk across a row of upturned knife-blades, each blade sharpened to the keenest edge, yet no sign of injury could be perceived on the naked foot. Another will climb a ladder formed of a single pole, from the sides of which well-sharpened sickles stand out to form the rungs. The fakir climbs to the top and descends. He rests his naked hands and feet upon the keen edges, and no cut, no mark can be seen; or he walks, still barefoot, over stones raised to white heat in a furnace. These feats have been performed in the presence of English gentlemen of high standing in the official world—men who have taken such precautions that they were perfectly certain that the feats were genuine—but they have been utterly unable to explain how the things were done. And, finally, the fakir has obtained such mastery of himself that he can be buried alive, being left for a time in his living grave, and restored to life again.

CHAPTER XVI

IN THE BAZAAR

WHAT is a bazaar in India? It is, first of all, the quarter where the shopkeepers are gathered together, where the tiny shops stand in close-packed rows on either side of the narrow ways, and whither all who have money flock to spend it. But it is more than that. It is the place to which those who have no money resort just as freely, for here ebbs and flows in one unending flood the news, the rumours, the gossip of the town and country.

All day long an Indian bazaar is filled with throngs of buyers, sellers, newsmongers, idle loungers, merchants, sightseers—all the flotsam and jetsam of the city. It is always a scene of wonderful colour and movement. The sun strikes into the dusty ways on turbans of red, green, and orange; on robes of white, pink and blue; on petticoats of rose and saffron; on the

A BAZAAR DELHI. *Chapter XIV.*

bronze bodies of almost naked coolies who march along beneath their loads. People of every colour—white, brown, black, yellow—jostle each other in the crowded ways, and there is a bewildering variety of tint and form in the striking and picturesque scene.

The shops are, as a rule, of the simplest nature in form—an archway, a booth, a hole in a wall. Upon a low platform the trader spreads his wares, squats beside them, and waits for customers. Let us stroll along a row of shops and see what they have for sale. The first shop has a crowd of customers, for it is a confectioner's, and the Hindoo, big or little, old or young, has a very sweet tooth. The confectioner spreads his wares on tiers of shelves or on a counter made of dried mud and rising in steps, and at the back of his shop is a sugar-boiling furnace, where he is busy on fresh supplies, pulling candy or making cakes of batter fried in butter. He sells toffee covered with silver-leaf, candy flavoured with spices, and many kinds of a sweet called luddu, made of sugar and curded milk. This stall is not only a great attraction to the children who have a pie (about one-third of an English farthing) to spend, but to the flies also. The latter come in myriads to settle on the sweet stuff, and though a boy is always at work with a whisk trying to drive them away, he can never keep the place clear.

Opposite the confectioner's is the flour-seller, and he, too, is a very busy man, for from his stall the everyday wants of the people are supplied. Great numbers of the Hindoos never touch meat, and the bunniah (the grain-seller) furnishes the whole of their food. He has a great number of baskets, and these are piled high with barley, wheat, lentils, flour, sugar, peas, rice, potatoes, nuts, dried fruits, and the like. He also sells ghee (clarified butter) and sour milk. He has a big pair of scales to weigh out his flour, sugar, peas, or whatever may be called for, but no bags to pack them in: he leaves that to the customers. One brings a cloth, another a basin, another a brass ewer for milk. Many have nothing, and they carry away their purchases in their hands, or, if that be impossible, flour is poured into the corner of a shawl or the fold of a robe. One man unwraps his turban and knots his purchases into various corners of it, twists it into shape again, and goes off with his day's supply on his head. Butter and milk are carried away in a green leaf dexterously twisted into the form of a cup.

The next shop is one which finds the grain-seller a very convenient neighbour, for it is a shop which sells parched grain—a bhunja's shop. At first glance there seems nothing in the place, then you notice a large shallow pan set on a mud platform. Under the pan a fire burns, and a woman steadily feeds the fire with dry leaves and husks. A second woman is stirring the corn in the pan, and as the grain parches and crackles a delicious smell fills the place, and passers-by sniff it, and stop and throw down a small copper coin on the mud platform, which is also the counter. Then they hold out their hands or a fold of a robe, and receive the sweet-smelling parched wheat or maize, and go on, munching as they walk.

Next comes a goldsmith's. Here is no glittering

shop with ornaments and precious vessels in the window, as in a London street, but an archway or a booth of mud exactly like his neighbours'. The goldsmith himself is at work with his blowpipe at a little brazier, softening and shaping a piece of gold into a bangle for a customer. He is a busy man, for the country women bring him their silver to be made up into the ornaments they love, and he has always a store of ear-rings and bracelets to sell.

He sells his goods by weight, and weighs them in a most delicate pair of scales, which he keeps in a sandal-wood box. His weights are the oddest things in the world—"tiny scraps of glass, a bean perhaps, an irregular chunk of some metal, a bit of stick, a red and black seed, an odd morsel of turquoise, and a thin leaf of mother-o'-pearl." His customers thus have to take the weight on his word ; and they do not always care about that, for, as the saying goes, a goldsmith would cheat his own mother on the scales. So that hot words often fly to and fro across the mud floor of his little shop, and passers-by pause to listen to the fierce dispute.

Beyond the goldsmith's stands the shop of a cloth merchant, and this is a very fine shop, one of the grandest in the bazaar. So large is the merchant's stock that his booth is really big, or he fills three or four archways with his piles of calico and woollen. Here you may buy the strong woollen and cotton cloths of the country, made well and dyed in quiet, tasteful colours—goods which will wash and wear for year after year. But, alas! you may also buy from an even greater store of the poorest and cheapest goods which Manchester can turn out—cottons which will be of the flimsiest as soon as the dressing is washed out of them, cheap gaudy woollens made of shoddy, and silks of no greater strength than the paper which enwraps them. For the craze for cheapness has invaded the Indian bazaar as elsewhere, and the splendid old silk muslins, the brocade which would last for a century, the woollen shawl that was handed down from mother to daughter, find few or no buyers nowadays.

The druggist (the pansari-ji) contents himself with one small room, but it is packed from floor to ceiling with a thousand odds and ends—drugs, medicines, spices, one can hardly tell what. He wraps his more precious wares in scraps of paper, and stows them away in baskets, boxes, pots, and pigeon-holes in the wall. He prides himself on keeping everything in stock in his line, and one writer speaks of testing a pansari-ji by asking for cuttle-fish bone, "and lo! there it was —just two or three small broken pieces in a paper screw." The druggist may be the doctor of his quarter as well, and a favourite method of cure will be to write a mysterious talisman on a scrap of paper or a betel-leaf. This is rolled into a pill and swallowed by the patient. Opium he sells largely, and at evening he dispenses the sleep-compelling drug to knot after knot of customers.

The fruit-dealer's shop makes a beautiful patch of colour in the bazaar, with its heaps of golden oranges, of purple plums, of speckled pomegranates, of jack-fruits and guavas, and many other kinds. But, as a rule, the fruit-dealers and greengrocers like a stall in a more open place, where they can pile their big melons up in a heap, and spread their wares in the lee of a wall, and throw an awning over to keep the sun off.

Now comes the cookshop, where rows of turbaned customers are squatted on the floor with bowls before them, and the busy cook is at work over a fireplace fed with dried leaves. He fries cakes of rice in oil, he spits half a dozen scraps of meat on a wooden skewer, and roasts them over charcoal. Then a big pot simmers over the fire of leaves, and the smell of a "double-onioned" stew is wafted across the place to mingle with a thousand other queer smells of the bazaar. He sells vegetables done up into all kinds of shapes, and made hot to the taste with plenty of curry ; he pickles carrots ; he has sweetmeats and great stores of pillau, a dish of meat cooked in rice. He has plenty of customers, for his prices are very low.

Then there is the kobariya, the marine-store dealer of the bazaar, whose shop is heaped with second-hand clothes, scrap-iron, and odds and ends. Mrs. Steel gives a vivid description of the wares of the kobariya :

"Old things, and still older things, upside down, higgledy-piggledy, hang on the top of each other : a patent rat-trap shouldering a broken lamp, an officer's tunic sheltering a pile of tent-pegs, a bazaar pipkin on top of some priceless old plate, a parrot's cage filled with French novels, a moth-eaten saddle keeping company with an old sword, and over all, sufficient scrap-iron to furnish forth a foundry ; and in an old caldron, incense spoons, little brass gods, prayer measures, sacred fire-holders, all mixed up with battered electro-plated forks, hot-water jug lids, and every conceivable kind of rubbish."

CHAPTER XVII

IN THE JUNGLE

The jungle, the Indian forest, is the home of many wild creatures, and the sportsman who goes into it in search of them often has to take his life in his hands. This is true, above all, if he is pursuing the tiger, the most ferocious beast that India knows, the king of the jungle. It is true, there are lions in India, but not many, and the Indian lion is of no great importance: the tiger is the beast of beasts.

The tiger is a terrible scourge to the Indian herdsman: a big brute will often take up his quarters near a village, and levy a regular toll on the village herds, killing cow after cow, and buffalo after buffalo. He is often perfectly well known, and the villagers see him about the roads, or crossing their fields, or gliding through the jungle without a sound on his soft pads. If a dozen of them are together they do not fear him: they march right through his haunts, shouting and singing, rattling sticks on the bamboo-trunks, and beating drums, and he gets out of the way and stops there. This is if he be an ordinary tiger, a cattle-killer; but if a man-eater haunts the neighbourhood, then the ryot's soul is filled with fear. He dares scarcely leave his house: to leave the village is to face a terrible danger; he knows not when the monster may steal upon him.

The man-eater goes about his work in dreadful silence. The ordinary tiger will often make the jungle ring again with his hoarse, deep roar; not so the man-eater. The latter glides without a sound, and under cover of a patch of bamboos or a clump of reeds, up to the wood-cutter felling a tree, or up to the peasant in his rice-field, or up to a woman fetching water from the well. Silent as death, he bounds upon his victims and fells them with a single stunning blow of that huge paw driven by muscles of steel. The great white fangs are buried for an instant in the throat, then the body is lifted in the mouth as a dog lifts a rat, and is carried away to the lair, where he makes his dreadful meal.

Most remarkable stories are told of the ferocity and daring of man-eating tigers. They have been known to venture boldly into a village by night and carry off sleepers who had sought a cool couch out of doors in the summer heats, and by day they have made fields and roads quite impossible places to venture into. Villages and whole tracts of country have at times been deserted by their inhabitants owing to the ravages of these ferocious creatures, and when an English sportsman arrives to tackle the savage beast he is hailed as a deliverer.

There are two favourite ways of hunting a tiger. The first depends on the fact that he must drink.

The sportsman, by means of native watchers, discovers the pool or water-hole where the tiger quenches his thirst. Then in a field near at hand is built a machan, a little platform where the hunter may watch and wait for his prey. He climbs into the machan at sunset, and waits till the tiger comes to drink at some time between the dark and the dawn, when a fortunate shot will put an end to the marauder.

The other way—a far more exciting and picturesque fashion—is to pursue the tiger upon elephants. The sportsmen are in open howdahs, and the elephants crash their way through the long grass, the reeds, the young bamboos, in search of the tiger. At last the tiger is driven into the open, and bullet after bullet is poured into his body by the marksmen. He is rarely killed at once, and in his agony he will often turn upon his pursuers with terrible fury. This is the moment of danger. With the horrible coughing roar of a charging tiger, he hurls himself with tremendous bounds upon his foes. His eyes blaze like green emeralds, his great fangs glitter like ivory. At springing distance he leaves the ground and shoots through the air like a thunderbolt, full upon the nearest elephant. Now is the time to try the sportsman's nerve and steadiness of aim. Unless the tiger be struck down by the heavy bullet, he will land with teeth and claws upon the flank of the elephant, striking and tearing with terrible effect at his foes.

More lives have been lost, however, by sportsmen following up a wounded tiger on foot. The tiger lies apparently stiff and still, as if already dead. The hunter

A NATIVE WOMAN WEARING NOSE ORNAMENT. *Page 57*

comes too near, and finds that there is a flicker of life left. Before he can retreat, the wounded beast puts forth its last strength to spring upon him and take a terrible revenge for its injuries.

We said that the tiger is the king of the Indian jungle. There are some observers who dispute this ; they award the palm to the elephant. Certainly there can be no more majestic sight than a herd of wild elephants in their native jungle. They move slowly along, staying now and again to crop the young shoots or to spout water over themselves at a pool or river. The huge grey bodies, on the round, pillar-like legs; the great flapping ears; the swinging, curling trunks; the rolling, lumbering walk, present a scene of great interest, heightened by the antics of the baby elephants, the calves, who trot along by their mothers and frisk around the herd.

The Indian elephant is rarely pursued and shot—it is far too valuable ; but the capture and taming of these mighty creatures is very exciting and interesting work. In Central India, especially in Mysore, their capture is usually carried out by means of a kheddah, a kind of pound. Two huge fences are built in the forest in the shape of a mighty V. The wide end of the V is often a mile or more across, and into this end a herd of wild elephants will be driven by great numbers of beaters. The elephants are urged forward to a large enclosure, into which the narrow end of the V opens. Once they are in this, a great gate is dropped behind them, and they are imprisoned.

Now the work of taming them begins. Tame

elephants take a great share in this, and show much cleverness in bringing their wild brethren into captivity. Two or three tame elephants, each with a driver on its back, will surround a wild one, and hustle and push it towards a strong tree. Now a man slips down from the back of a tame elephant, and slips a noose of strong rope round the leg of the wild one. This is dangerous work, and the man has to be very quick and skilful. The rope is now thrown round the tree, and drawn tight. Other ropes are soon fastened, and the huge wild creature is made a prisoner.

The task of taming him at once begins. From the first the men move about the captive and talk to him, to accustom him to their sight and presence. They give him plenty of nice things to eat, and from the first he does not refuse food, except in very rare cases. Very often within a couple of days the elephant is taking pieces of sugar-cane and fruit from the hands of his keepers. Now the friendship grows rapidly. The men begin to pat and caress the huge captive as they sing and talk to him, and within a couple of weeks his bonds are loosened, and he is led away between two tame companions to complete his education.

There is one elephant that no one tries, or dares to try, to capture. This is the "rogue," and he is pursued and shot at once, if possible. A rogue elephant is a savage, vicious brute who has left the herd and taken to a solitary life. They are very dangerous, and many of them will attack either man or beast that may come in their way. Their great size and vast strength render them easy conquerors over all they meet, and a rogue elephant is the dread of the neighbourhood where he roams. To hunt him is a very dangerous sport. He is very wary, very cunning, and quite fearless. If fired upon he charges full upon his foes, and, unless a well-directed bullet brings him down, the death of the hunter is certain. The rogue hurls him down and tramples upon him, smashing the body beneath his huge feet.

CHAPTER XVIII

IN THE JUNGLE (*continued*)

THROUGH the jungle bound also the swift deer and the graceful antelopes, who so often have to fly before the pursuit of their fierce neighbours the tiger and the panther. The panther, when wounded, is actually more feared by the hunter than is the tiger. The panther is much smaller than the tiger, and his grey skin, dotted with black spots, enables him to hide himself easily among the tangle of the forest undergrowth, for he resembles a patch of shade. His limbs are long and powerful, and he is the nimblest of all the jungle dwellers. He can run like a leopard and climb like a monkey.

He often lies in wait for his prey on a broad, low-hanging branch; then, as the deer passes below, he springs full upon it, and bears it to the ground. He is very savage, and always full of fight, and his ferocity is employed with wonderful cunning. Two men have been known to fire upon a panther and hit it. They were apparently safe, each in a machan set in a tall tree. The wounded brute has darted up one tree and clawed the man there in fearful fashion ; then, quick as lightning, it has descended, climbed into the second tree, and attacked its second assailant. No other animal does this. As a rule, a wounded beast makes a blind rush ; but the panther seems to reason, to calculate.

The bear is just the opposite. The natives consider him the most stupid of animals. They say he is so stupid that he does not know enough to get out of the way. He will stretch himself in the warm dust of a jungle path, and lie there until, in the dusk, the passer-by stumbles over him. Then he is angry. He rises and strikes out with his long claws, and often deals terrible wounds, for he strikes at the head. One writer speaks of seeing a man whose face was torn away—every feature gone—with a single stroke of a bear's paw. But it is easy to avoid this. On such a path a native sings or shouts as he walks along. The bear is aroused by the noise, and moves away into the jungle.

The wild boar gives great sport over the plains and among the hills of India. He is hunted on horseback, just as the fox is hunted in England, save that each rider has a spear with which to strike at the big, savage beast. When he turns at bay he is a very dangerous animal. First he "squats"—that is, he turns round and sits on his haunches—thrusting out his snout, armed with great sharp tusks, towards his pursuers. Then he picks out a horseman, and charges him furiously. A fine hand with a spear will now stop him with a thrust in a vital part; but if the thrust fails, the boar will often fetch down horse and rider.

Then comes a time of great danger, for the boar will rip up both horse and man with swift turns of his keen tusks unless his attention be drawn aside by other attacks. In the end he falls under many spear-thrusts.

A walk through an open piece of jungle is very beautiful. The bamboos with their feathery crowns, the many trees covered with beautiful flowers, the merry bands of monkeys which skip from branch to branch, all draw the eye and the attention; but, at the same time, it is best to watch where you are going.

All of a sudden your native guide stops you and tells you to step carefully. You look, and see something in the path among the sand looking like a dirty little stick. But do not tread on it. It is the deadliest snake in India, and its bite means certain death. Or you think you would like to sit down on a fallen tree to rest. Well, do not sit on that log which seems to have a bright patch of fungus growing about the middle of it. Throw a stick at the patch first. Ah! it uncoils, and a venomous reptile slides into the grass with angry hiss.

Look out, too, for the hooded cobra, who will sometimes dispute the way with you, rearing himself on his lower coils, and erecting his swelling hood, and "meaning venom." But the most wonderful snake of all is the huge python, the boa-constrictor, 20 to 25 feet long, and with a body as thick as a man's thigh. This huge snake destroys its prey by pressure, winding its coils round the creature's body, and crushing it to death. Then it swallows the body entire.

Another creature greatly dreaded by the natives belongs partly to the land and partly to the water. This is the alligator—a hideous grey brute, with huge jaws, furnished with long rows of teeth, and a long tail of immense power. On land the natives trouble little about this great reptile, for his legs are short and his powers of pursuit are small; but in the water or on the sandy margin it is a very different affair. Be careful where you bathe or draw water. A single sweep of that powerful tail will hurl you into the stream, and the alligator, lurking in the shallows, has seized you for his prey. Above all, it is necessary to be careful when walking along the pleasant sandy bank which often borders a river. Here and there grey logs seem to be lying on the sand. They may be logs or they may be alligators sunning themselves. In the latter case, if the walker be on the land side, well and good; but if he incautiously ventures between the alligator and the river, it is at the peril of his life. With the aid of his powerful tail, the frightful reptile hurls himself across the sand for a short distance at wonderful speed, then his mighty jaws open and close upon his victim, and the latter is dragged under water in the twinkling of an eye.

The tiger himself, unmatched in combat with any other beast of the jungle, sometimes falls a prey to the alligator. Coming to drink at the river, the king of the jungle is seized by the waiting reptile. A terrific struggle follows. Unable to wrench himself from those mighty jaws, the tiger uses his terrible fangs and claws on the alligator's back. Here for once they fail on that coat of horny scales. The tiger does not know that the alligator is soft beneath, and there could be ripped up by his claws of steel, and he continues to spend his strength in vain. Inch by inch he is dragged into the river, and once under water, he is lost. He swiftly drowns, and the alligators feast on his body.

CHAPTER XIX

IN AN INDIAN VILLAGE

We have spoken of temples and palaces and the magnificence of Kings and nobles, but now we must turn to the homes of the common people, and see how they live and work. Anyone who adopted the idea that India is a land of general riches and splendour would be making a very great mistake. The vast mass of the people live, not merely in the simplest fashion, but also in the poorest fashion, for the land can scarce produce enough food to satisfy the wants of its teeming millions. If the rains should fail and a crop go wrong, there is famine at once over wide districts, and vast numbers perish.

An Indian village is a collection of small huts, with walls of mud and roof of thatch. At break of day the men, the ryots, go out to labour in the fields which surround the place, putting their bullocks into the light wooden plough, which scarcely does more than scratch the soil. In the shallow furrow thus formed they sow the grain, and then with hoe and mattock they clean the weeds from a crop which is already springing up. These few simple tools serve all the purposes of the husbandman, just as they served his forefathers a thousand years ago.

The women of the village go to the well to draw water, passing on their way the village temple, where they offer fruits and flowers to the stone image of the Hindoo god, in whose honour the temple was built. When they have drawn their water, they return home to cook food and to work in the small compound which surrounds each mud hut. Here they grow trees, which yield the mango, plantain, guava, and other fruits.

As they go back to their homes they cast looks of deep interest at the door of a house where a figure is seated. It is a Brahmin sitting in dharna, for this is an out-of-the-way village where old customs cling fast.

What is dharna? It is really a form of intimidation. Some one has a quarrel with the owner of that house, and he has hired a Brahmin, a member of the priestly caste, to sit on his enemy's doorstep without food or drink, until the latter will do justice. The Brahmin, having undertaken the task, is certain to carry it through. He will starve until the person at whose door he sits has given way. The latter always happens. If the holy man were to starve to death, the sin would

A NATIVE BULLOCK CART. *Page 80.*

lie upon the head of the owner of the house for ever, and his fate in the next world would be dreadful. So, before long, some arrangement is made, and the dispute is settled.

The house before which the Brahmin is performing dharna is that of the money-lender, by far the most powerful man in the village. When a ryot cannot make both ends meet, and he is in trouble either about his rent or his taxes, it is to the money-lender that he flies for assistance. From that powerful personage he borrows a few rupees to tide him over the time of need till his crops shall be ready for sale, and he has to pay a very heavy rate of interest for the loan.

The money-lender is one of the oldest features of Indian village life. From the earliest times his trade has been in great vogue, and the Indian peasant is to-day as dependent upon him as ever. Broadly speaking, the ryot is always in debt. He is so careless, and thinks so little of the future that he always lives from hand to mouth, and a failure of his crop brings him within touch of famine at once. Then he resorts to the money-lender to borrow money to buy food or pay his rent, and to raise the money he often agrees to sell his next crop to the money-lender at a price which the money-lender himself will fix.

The price is very low, and the money is at once swallowed up to pay rent or the interest on the last loan, and so the peasant is driven to apply to the money-lender once more to obtain funds to carry him on to the next harvest. In this way the ryot falls completely into the hands of the money-lender, and, in order that the unlucky husbandman may not escape his clutches, the creditor employs men to watch the farmer's crops day and night, and the latter has to pay all these expenses.

Just beyond the money-lender's house is the dwelling of the baid, the doctor. He is sitting on his veranda, busily reading a very ancient book on medicine. It is from the instructions in this book that he treats all his patients. He has a store of herbs and roots, which he uses to make pills and potions. He looks with the greatest contempt on the European doctors and their medicines, and declares that they do not know how to treat Hindoo patients.

As a rule, the baid is a very poor hand at curing his patients. If they get well he takes all the credit; if they die he says that the hour of their death had come, and who can resist fate? But here and there are to be found men who have so great a knowledge of herbs and simples that they can effect wonderful cures. "A curious cure of asthma is recorded of a European who derived little benefit from the treatment of his own countrymen. A baid offered to cure him when his case had become almost hopeless. The European laughed. However, getting quite desperate, he submitted to the treatment of the Hindoo doctor, and the few sweet black pills which the latter administered wrought a complete cure. The grateful patient begged the doctor to name his own reward; but he would listen to nothing of the kind, nor would he tell of what ingredients the pills were composed. Indeed, this the baids will never do."

In an Indian Village

CHAPTER XX

IN AN INDIAN VILLAGE (*continued*)

Now there comes up to the veranda a quiet-looking man with a little bundle under his arm, and the baid lays aside his book. The village barber has come to shave him. The Hindoo barber is a very important man. Not only has he under his care the shaven crowns, the smooth chins, and the close-cropped hair of his neighbours, but he is the village surgeon also, for the baid knows nothing of surgery. It is the barber who bores the ears and noses of the little girls to put in rings and ornaments.

He squats down beside the doctor and unrolls his little bundle and spreads out its contents. He has a razor, a pair of scissors, a small steel instrument for cutting nails, a leather strop, a little brass cup, a scrap of looking-glass, and a towel. He uses neither brush nor soap for shaving, but puts cold water in the cup and dips his fingers into it. With these fingers he wets and rubs the chin, and then sweeps his razor over it with light and skilful hand, doing his work like a master. When he has finished he rolls up his little bundle and goes on to the next house, for he has a fixed round of customers, and no Hindoo, whether rich or poor, ever shaves himself.

Going thus from house to house the barber knows every one, and is often employed as a match-maker.

In India parents always arrange the marriages of their children, and the wishes of the latter are not consulted in the affair. Indeed, marriages are often settled at so early an age that the children do not understand what it means. A girl is fetched from her play and married to a boy not much older than herself. She goes back to her dolls, and he goes back to school, and perhaps neither sees the other again for years.

In arranging these affairs there is often much coming and going of the family barber. He has to find out how much dowry the parents of the girl will give with their daughter, or, on the other hand, he is sent to see what examinations the young man has passed. This is an important point. The Hindoos think a great deal of such distinctions, and a young man who has passed a University examination can get a much richer wife than he who has not.

At the wedding the barber is a very busy man. Before the day he goes round to the friends and relatives of the family inviting them to come to the wedding-feast, and begging them not to fail in attendance. On the day of the wedding he has to dress the bridegroom, and when the guests are assembled he hands round betels to chew or hookahs to smoke. He helps to serve the wedding-feast, and when it is over he distributes the fragments among the beggars.

The barber's wife is as important a personage as himself. She is just as busy among the women as he is among the men. She enters the zenana, the women's portion of the house, to dress the ladies and adorn them. At weddings she dresses the hair of the bride, trims her nails, and arrays her in the richest robes.

Both the barber and his wife belong to the barber caste. In India trades are handed down from father to son, from mother to daughter. The children of the barber and his wife are taught from their earliest years the duties of their business: they, too, will become barbers in due time.

As the barber goes away the water-carrier comes up. This is another important personage; for, in the burning climate of India, fresh, pure water is of the greatest importance. This water-carrier has not filled his vessels at the village well, but has been to a spring at some distance, where the water is very good. He carries it in two large vessels of brass, and these are slung from the ends of a pole which he carries across one of his shoulders, one vessel in front and one behind.

If there are Mohammedans in the village you will also see the bhistee, the Mohammedan water-carrier. He bears his load in a skin on his shoulders, or in a pair of skins which he slings across the back of a bullock. He sells water only to people of his own faith, for no Hindoo will use for any purpose water which a Mohammedan has handled.

The larger houses have flat roofs, and from the roofs of two standing near each other a couple of boys are having a battle with fighting kites. Flying kites is a very favourite amusement in India, and in some villages old and young, rich and poor, spend much time on this sport. The kites are square in shape, but of all sizes, and in the case of fighting kites the string or thread is passed through a mixture of pounded glass and starch and then dried. The thread has now a keen, cutting edge, and if brought sharply across the string of another kite will cut it through, and he who succeeds in setting his opponent's kite adrift is the victor.

At the farther end of our village there is a large native inn. This is by no means a common thing to find in such a place ; but, as it happens, a well-travelled road passes through the country at this point. To see this inn at its busiest we must go on some evening when a fair is to be held in the neighbouring town, and a throng of travellers pause in it for the night.

The inn itself, as we approach it, shows a square of four flat naked walls. There are neither doors nor windows to be seen, and the place is entered by a wide opening, which can be closed by massive gates. Near the gate are some small shops where one can buy rice, flour, salt, and ghee to eat, or earthen pots for cooking.

Upon entering, we find ourselves in a big courtyard, the middle of which is packed with the bullock waggons and carts, from which the ponies and bullocks have just been released and turned out to graze. Round the walls inside is a wide veranda, and behind this veranda are rooms wherein the wayfarers may sleep. The scene is one of the greatest uproar and confusion. Men and women are bustling to and fro, shouting and calling to each other as they draw water, light fires, cook food, feed their animals, spread their beds, and generally make ready for the night.

Every inch of the veranda is taken up, and in front of each room burns the fire of the party who intend to occupy it. A wealthy traveller will engage a number of rooms for himself and his family or servants ; but poor men club together, and five or six engage a single room and stow themselves away in it. The cost to them will then be about one farthing per head.

The inn is under the charge of a number of inn-keepers, each of whom has a certain part of the inn-yard under his care and a certain number of rooms to let. These people crowd about the traveller on his arrival, each clamouring that his rooms are the best, and begging for his custom. They are a thievish and quarrelsome crew, and are looked down upon as a very low and degraded class. In a native inn the traveller has to keep a very sharp eye on his belongings. He takes care to keep his money in a safe place, and he never accepts tobacco or any eatable from a stranger. There may be a drug in it which will throw him into a deep sleep, from which he will awake to find all his valuables gone.

When supper is dispatched the traveller prepares for sleep. If poor, he stretches himself on the floor; if better off, he hires a wooden frame from the inn-keeper, and spreads upon it his quilts and blankets. Now the great gates are swung to and locked, and the inn is securely shut up for the night. This is very necessary, or some of the animals would be missing in the morning. There are also men who keep watch all night, and the merchant with a stock of valuable goods gives one of these a small sum to take particular care of his bales and animals.

BILLING AND SONS, LTD., PRINTERS, GUILDFORD.